A HISTORY
of LONDON *in*
50 LIVES

A HISTORY
of LONDON *in*
50 LIVES

DAVID LONG

A Oneworld Book

Published in North America, Great Britain
and Australia by Oneworld Publications, 2015
Reprinted, 2023

ISBN 978–1–78074–570–1
eISBN 978–1–78074–571–8

Text designed and typeset by Tetragon, London
Printed and bound in Great Britain by Clays Ltd, Elcograf S.p.A

Oneworld Publications
10 Bloomsbury Street
London WC1B 3SR
England

Stay up to date with the latest books,
special offers, and exclusive content from
Oneworld with our newsletter

Sign up on our website
oneworld-publications.com

MIX
Paper from
responsible sources
FSC® C018072

CONTENTS

Contents

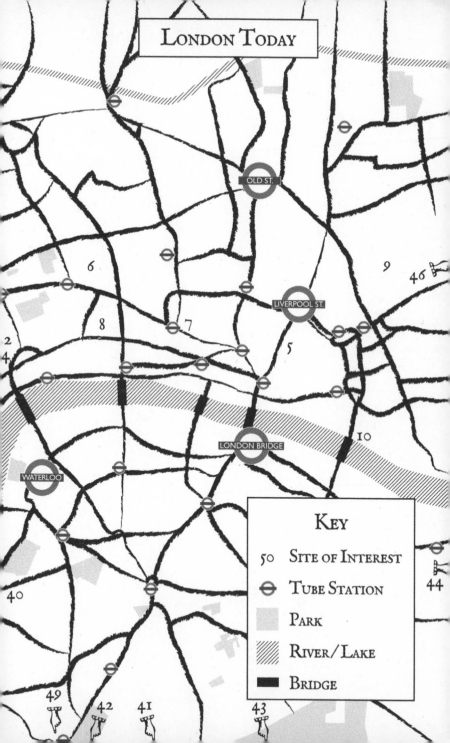

INTRODUCTION

*'It is not the walls that make the city, but the
people who live within them.'*

GEORGE VI

For all the noble churches and superb buildings
that James Boswell observed on his arrival in
eighteenth-century London, the fact that he
noted the 'variety of perfect and curious characters'
is a reminder that a city, any city, is nothing without its
citizens. And assuming one accepts Disraeli's famous
description of the heart of the British Empire a hundred
years later – as somewhere that provided 'a roost for every
bird' – then London can fairly be said to have been the
birthplace or the destination for birds of every feather.

Choosing only a few dozen of them one cannot hope
to tell the full story, but that was never the intention
behind this book. Nor is *A History of London in 50 Lives* an
attempt to describe only the most illustrious, notorious
or obscure Londoners. Instead it comprises a personal
selection of some of the more interesting figures from the

last few hundred years: heroes and villains; well-known names alongside others who are far less so; men and women who were born in London and helped make it great, or those who came here from elsewhere and were themselves made by their time spent in this truly unique and special city.

Reading the stories of any of these figures it is clear that however you view the place – as Disraeli's modern Babylon, Arthur Conan Doyle's great cesspool, or as it was for Herman Melville somewhere a man could easily disappear – King George was right. London's story is the story of Londoners, born, made or adopted, and always was.

DAVID LONG
www.davidlong.info

Chapter 1

MAYFAIR AND ST JAMES'S

1. Napoleon III (1808–73)

1c King Street, SW1

The oldest shop in London is that of the hat maker James Lock in St James's Street, and the second-oldest the wine merchants a few doors down the hill. Lettering outside Berry Bros. & Rudd proudly states 'established in XVIIth Century', and inside the panelled premises of the eighth-generation family firm are giant leather-bound ledgers containing the personal details of many distinguished customers including Lord Byron, Beau Brummell, George IV, King Louis-Philippe and Napoleon III. [*]

---

[*] Lock's record keeping is similarly meticulous, and today the staff are able instantly to lay their hands on the hat measurements of, say, Lord Nelson or the Duke of Wellington.

The idea of a Frenchman buying wine in London (let alone a French king or an emperor) seems extraordinary until one walks around the corner into King Street. There, a nineteenth-century wall plaque – the only one in London to include the French imperial eagle – confirms that Napoleon III was not simply a customer but also one of the locals.

As Prince Louis Napoleon, Bonaparte's nephew and heir, he spent some years living in exile in St James's, initially in Carlton House Terrace and then Carlton Gardens before taking on the lease of a new house in King Street in 1847. This was expensively fitted out as a shrine to his uncle, a place to display a large collection of various uniforms and other relics of Bonaparte's ill-fated adventures across Europe. London looked on somewhat bemused, but as the young Frenchman seemed to pose no threat he was invited into society, while members of the Army & Navy Club (aka 'The Rag') on Pall Mall granted him honorary membership.

More surprising, perhaps, as Europe was being rocked by revolution and London was hit by the Chartist riots of 1848, the future emperor enrolled briefly as a 'special' (an unpaid part-time police officer) before resigning and returning to France.

He was elected president of the short-lived Second Republic the same year, and then following a coup d'état in 1851 and the creation of the Second Empire he ruled for nearly twenty years as Napoleon III. As the last Emperor of the French he enjoyed some success domestically, and sensibly proclaimed that *L'Empire, c'est la paix* ('the Empire means peace'). Unfortunately he was unable to hold to this maxim, and proceeded to fight a great number of wars and on a mammoth scale – in the Crimea, Italy, Mexico, against Prussia and even Korea.

At one point he considered intervening for the Confederacy in the American Civil War, but inevitably it all proved too much. When the events of the Franco-Prussian War led to Napoleon III's ignominious surrender at Sedan in 1870 – and at least forty thousand French casualties – the humiliation of being captured

APRES MOI, L'OMELETTE

The last French monarch was by no means the only one to settle on British soil. The 'citizen-king' Louis Philippe spent fifteen years living in England: briefly resident in Bury St Edmunds, he moved to Surrey where he died in 1850. Before this Louis XVIII had leased Hartwell House in Buckinghamshire from 1809–14, a place so far beyond his means – despite being broke he arrived with a retinue of at least a hundred hangers-on – that he was forced to keep a flock of chickens. These he kept on the roof in order to prevent the various impecunious French nobles living in the surrounding cowsheds and pigsties from pinching his eggs.

proved such a disaster nationally and personally that once released he was forced back into exile and fled back to London.

Six months living as a German captive had left Napoleon a bitter, broken man, and for the remainder of his life – spent in England, with his wife Eugenie and his son – he was haunted by such regrets and memories of defeat that his last words (whispered to a doctor called to his deathbed) were '*Etiez-vous à Sedan?*' – were you at Sedan?

By this time the family, still very much insisting on the privileges of an imperial family, were settled at Camden Place in what is now Chislehurst, a suburb of Bromley. Napoleon was finished with society, and society was clearly finished with him, and two years after his return Napoleon III was laid to rest at the Catholic church of St Mary's, Chislehurst.

There is a strange footnote to the story. His widow, refusing to relinquish her husband's imperial ambitions – and hit hard by their son's death (while fighting for the British in the Zulu Wars) – decided to found a monastery at Farnborough in Hampshire. Intended for monks driven out of France by the anti-clerical edicts of the Third Republic, the plans included an imperial crypt to which the bodies of her husband and the so-called Prince Imperial were brought in 1888. Their tombs, and her own, can still be seen on public days, the monks staunchly defending recent moves from France to have all three bodies repatriated nearly a century and a half after they were sent into exile.

2. Harry Gordon Selfridge (1858-1947)

9 Fitzmaurice Place, Berkeley Square, W1

'Only X shopping days before Christmas' is a phrase to cheer the heart or chill the bones, depending on your mood. Either way, it was coined by the American-born retail magnate Harry Gordon Selfridge, one of many snappy and effective marketing slogans he came up with – 'the customer is never wrong' is thought to be another – most of which were quickly borrowed and adapted by his rivals.

A partner in the US giant Marshall Field (still with us, as part of the Macy's and Bloomingdale's empire) Selfridge and his wife arrived in Mayfair in the early 1900s. Unimpressed by the quality of London department stores he decided to establish his own, ploughing an estimated £400,000 (equivalent to more than £120 million today) into a large plot on what was then a decidedly unfashionable stretch of Oxford Street. The result was the building familiar to visitors today, its giant Ionic columns the work of architects R.F. Atkinson and Thomas Smith Tait (and influenced by those of an Edwardian extension to the British Museum). A clock forms its centrepiece, nearly three and a half metres in diameter and called *The Queen of Time.*

Selfridge's own sense of timing was impeccable, and in the early days he was a canny and highly perceptive operator. An early advocate of paid advertising, he also recognized that a generation of newly emancipated women looked upon shopping as a recreation not a chore, and so worked tirelessly to promote Selfridges as a destination rather than a mere shop. He also lobbied hard to get the nearest underground station renamed Selfridges, and even when his friend Lord Ashfield, managing director of the Underground Electric Railway Company, decided to stick with the name Bond Street serious consideration was given to running a private tunnel from the escalators right into the store.

Selfridge was also a great innovator. In 1910 his emporium became the first in the world to have a ground floor beauty department, and today – when almost every rival has followed suit – its beauty hall is still the world's largest (it sells more than 7,700 lipsticks, 2,800 mascaras and 1,000 nail polishes every week). For years the store ran its own private Information Bureau, equipped with more books than many borough libraries and with a trained

SELFRIDGE SEES THE LIGHT

Selfridge frequently called on new technologies to boost his business. In 1909 Louis Blériot's aeroplane went on display in the store shortly after the Frenchman had become the first to fly across the English Channel, and more than 150,000 Londoners queued up to see it. In 1925 the Scottish inventor John Logie Baird was paid £25 per week to demonstrate his new machine to customers, Selfridge seeing at once that what its creator called the 'Televisor' was not simply a toy but 'a link between all peoples of the world'. Four years later, to celebrate the store's twentieth anniversary, the exterior was lit up by an unprecedented display of more than thirty thousand electric light bulbs. And in 2000, to mask the scaffolding while its huge façade was being restored, Selfridges commissioned the world's largest and longest ever photograph from artist Sam Taylor-Wood. Nearly one thousand feet long, the artist's modern interpretation of the Parthenon frieze depicted twenty-one contemporary personalities, including Elton John, the actress Jane Horrocks and the dancer Stephen Galloway.

staff dedicated to finding answers to literally any question a customer might put to them. Movie directors were also invited to film scenes in the store, providing yet more valuable publicity for the company, as indeed they still are. (A recent memorable example is Richard Curtis's hit *Love Actually* in 2003, in which Rowan Atkinson's maddeningly meticulous service after he enquires of Alan Rickman's agitated customer 'Would you like it gift wrapped?' beautifully demonstrates the accessible luxury of the Selfridges experience.)

Already rich when he arrived in London the popularity and runaway success of the new venture made Selfridge richer still, and following the death of his wife (in the 1918 flu pandemic) he settled down to enjoy it in fine Mayfair style. For a while he flirted with the idea of building a huge square tower on top of the store, one that would have dominated the whole of the West End had not his architect warned that it was so massive that the entire edifice would have collapsed under its own weight.

Instead, in the absence of such an obvious monument, a Blue Plaque at 9 Fitzmaurice Place is now all there is to give one an indication of the scale on which he chose to spend his fortune. Today home to the Lansdowne Club, this was once a truly magnificent Adam mansion with wings either side of the main Palladian block and private gardens so extensive that even into the twentieth century it could still be described as 'secluded'. The house had been built for the fabulously rich Marquess of Bute (1713–92), Britain's first Scottish prime minister, but was then sold to William, Earl of Shelburne who renamed it after himself when he was created Marquess of Lansdowne.

Its façade and wings have since been demolished to make way for a road cut through from Berkeley Square to Curzon Street and Piccadilly in the 1930s. When Selfridge took over the lease in 1921, however, Robert Adam's masterpiece was still very much one of the great houses of Mayfair, and Selfridge's period as its custodian was to scandalize London society. (Even more so, it was said, than his decision in 1922 to dress his waitresses in racy trouser suits instead of skirts so that they could hurry more quickly to and from the kitchen.)

The cause of the scandal this time was his love life, which included affairs with a divorcée (heiress Syrie Barnardo Wellcome, who later married the writer Somerset Maugham) and the Dolly Sisters, a fashionable pair of cabaret artistes of middle-European origins. The idea of cabaret girls was in itself sufficient to make many a dowager feel faint; what made Selfridge's behaviour even more *outré* was that when discreet enquiries were made to determine which sister he was actually having the affair with – Jenny or Rosie – all the evidence seemed to suggest that he was carrying on with both of them simultaneously.

While the girls gambled recklessly, Selfridge spent in much the same wild manner on lavish parties. Fleets of Rolls-Royces were used to ferry his friends to race meetings and country house weekends, and for a while he even entertained a truly mad plan to build himself a castle in Hampshire surrounded by more than four miles of high stone wall.

It was all so deliciously decadent, typically 1920s and oh-so-Mayfair, but also horrifyingly expensive. Unfortunately, taking his eye off the ball in this way also meant that control of Oxford Street's mightiest retail phenomenon gradually slipped from its founder's grasp and, deftly outmanoeuvred by his fellow directors, he was drummed out of the firm. With his fortune further diminished by the Depression of the 1930s, the great Harry Gordon Selfridge, incredibly, fell into debt. In 1947 he died a poor man, living in a tiny flat across the river in Putney.

3. Nancy Astor (1879-1964)

4 St James's Square, SW1

The second lady MP and the first to take her seat in Parliament, Lady Astor was such an energetic Hitler appeaser, so famously stern and aggressively teetotal that it is tempting to wonder what she would make of her London home these days. No. 4 St James's Square, a precious and unique early eighteenth-century survivor complete with an extensive garden and its own mews, is

MAKE MINE A DOUBLE

They say you can tell a man (or woman) by the company he keeps, but not all of Nancy Astor's house guests respected her high-minded stance on the drinking of alcohol. The notorious British fascist leader Sir Oswald Mosley and his wife were good friends but routinely smuggled in a secret supply of Martinis whenever they came to stay. Another guest – the reviled Nazi diplomat Joachim von Ribbentrop, who for a while lived round the corner in Carlton House Terrace – was previously employed as a champagne salesman.

now home to the Naval & Military Club. There are today a few female members, it is true, but most of the members in the club's illustrious 150-year history have been chaps, the vast majority coming to sit in one of its three bars, order a round of drinks and enjoy each other's company. Very few, one suspects, would have been in favour of sitting down for a parley with Mr Hitler.

Nancy and her husband Waldorf, 2nd Viscount Astor were in residence for much of the first half of the twentieth century however, using the house as their London base and a refuge from the improvements being carried out at Cliveden, their country home on the banks of the Thames. (Keen to keep the public out of the estate after buying it from the 2nd Duke of Westminster, Astor became known to locals by the nickname 'Walled-Orf'.)

As well as an obvious meeting place for what became known as the Cliveden Set, a group of prominent right-wing Germanophiles keen to foster friendly relations with Hitler and his circle, the spacious London house was an essential adjunct to Nancy's parliamentary career. Convenient for the Palace of Westminster, it was also sufficiently grand to enable her to play the role of political hostess at what was to become one of the more significant, if controversial, political *salons* of the 1930s. To accomplish all this required a considerable fortune, which luckily the Waldorf inheritance was able to supply – but also Nancy's very considerable drive and intelligence.

Once in Parliament Lady Astor achieved relatively little of lasting note, never holding high office and today being remembered more for being elected than for her achievements once she was sworn in. She was nevertheless a fascinating individual, and a mass of intriguing contradictions. Personally she was actively religious, somewhat reserved and something of a prude; yet in public her conversation was sharply witty and frequently quite saucy. Like her husband she was an American through and through, but like Waldorf she slipped happily into English habits, and clearly enjoyed the culture and accoutrements of a traditional Edwardian's aristocratic way of life.

As a Christian Scientist Nancy did not approve of medical intervention, yet she was happy for Cliveden to be used during the Second World War as a hospital for wounded

Canadian soldiers. Similarly, whilst she was absolutely one of the genuine pioneers when it came to advancing the cause of women in politics, she was regarded as out of touch by the women of the suffragette movement and as being too upper class. But perhaps most worrying of all was that towards the end of the war, having acknowledged that she and her fellow appeasers had been wrong to call for peace talks with the Nazis, she stigmatized the 8th Army, Britain's legendary Desert Rats.

Calling them 'D-Day dodgers' in a public speech, suggesting they had ducked the real war in France in favour of a softer option, she also went to great lengths to express a preference for First World War wounded whenever she was confronted by the injured of the Second World War.

Inevitably such views did not endear her to the voting public, and by the time her husband persuaded her to step down in 1945 the Tory Party had already come to regard her increasingly as an electoral liability. Thereafter, her long-standing antipathy towards Catholics – including her own daughter-in-law – came to embrace many other ethnic and religious minorities.

New York, she felt, had become too 'Jewish and foreign', and on at least one occasion she told a group of African Americans that they should be grateful for the slave trade as it had been their path to Christianity. (A class of black students were likewise advised to try to become more like the servants she remembered from her own childhood, an especially obnoxious comment coming from the daughter of a slave owner.)

Having also fallen out with her husband when his own politics gradually shifted to the left, her later years saw her become a bitter and solitary old lady. This was perhaps no more than she deserved, although as she preferred to see it, 'Pioneers may be picturesque figures, but they are often rather lonely ones.'

4. Jimi Hendrix (1942–70) & George Frideric Handel (1685–1759)

23 Brook Street, W1

Hendrix famously died in a bedroom at the exotically named Samarkand Hotel at 22 Lansdowne Crescent, W11 but for two key years in his brief, meteoric career he lived in Mayfair, occupying a small flat in part of what for nearly forty years had been the home of the royal *kapellmeister* George Frideric Handel.

It is said that when the gifted but impressionable young American discovered that some crazy famous classical cat had lived and composed in the very same building, he went straight out and bought a copy of the *Messiah*. He reportedly played the record over and over, and even now some amateur musicologists claim to find parallels between sequences in Handel's great work and particular riffs on some of their hero's London recordings.

At the time of Handel's death in 1759 in a first-floor bedroom, he and his family had been paying £60 a year for what was then quite a substantial terraced property. That he was buried in Westminster Abbey speaks volumes for the high regard in which he was held, an accolade only slightly spoiled by the decision of the sculptor Louis-François Roubiliac to model the ears of his effigy on those belonging to a young lady friend because, as an artist, he found the size and form of Handel's own ears to be unacceptable.

In Germany nearly half a century earlier Handel had secured the post of chapel master to Georg, Elector of Hanover. In 1714 the prince became King George I of Great Britain and Ireland, by which time Handel was already calling Mayfair home and living on a pension of £200 per year from Queen Anne.

Handel's assimilation into London society was rapid and total, with commissions from many nobles, important duties at the new Royal Academy of Music, and prestigious performances of his work each year for the Foundling Hospital. Indeed, many of his compositions are now so ingrained in the British national psyche – besides popular favourites such as the *Messiah* and his *Water Music*, Handel's *Zadok the Priest* has been performed at every

JIMI'S FIRST AND LAST

Hendrix's last London gig is a matter of record: it was at Ronnie Scott's in Soho, where he sat in with Eric Burdon's band War a couple of nights before he died. His first gig is far harder to prove with any certainty, although a leading contender is a club called The Scotch of St James. Situated just off St James's Square in Mason's Yard, this was a small but well-known 1960s landmark. Everyone from The Beatles to The Who played the intimate basement at some time or other and it is thought to have been the location of Jimi's first impromptu gig, which followed his arrival in England in 1966.

coronation since 1727 – that it is sometimes forgotten that he was German by birth.

Some time after his death the property was subdivided into two houses (now Nos. 23 and 25) and later still into shops and several smaller dwellings. Hendrix and his girlfriend Kathy Etchingham moved into one of the latter in 1968, paying £30 per week for what in Handel's day would have been a couple of servants' rooms in the attic. Hendrix loved it, calling the little garret 'the first little home of my own', and when possible the two of them would watch *Coronation Street,* Jimi being something of an Ena Sharples fan. When he died on 18 September 1970 his name was still on the lease.

With its twin Blue Plaques (Jimi's being the first one to commemorate a rock-and-roll star) the building provides a more solid link between the two musicians than the aforementioned riffs, as well as making a pairing that is sufficiently unexpected as to charm many passers-by. Unlike a lot of the buildings in this book, this one can actually be visited, and a painstaking restoration of the half that is now the Handel House Museum means it gives one a fine impression of how it must have appeared in the 1750s.

The restoration of Handel's house means, of course, that there is no longer any trace of Hendrix or of Kathy – the attic is now used for administration and storage – although in 2010 the museum put on a temporary exhibition of Jimi memorabilia, including one of his trademark soft felt hats, a sunburst orange jacket, travel directions to the Isle of Wight (for the festival) and, perhaps the best of all, a small fragment of paper torn from a pad at the Hyde Park Towers hotel on which are written a few lines from 'Third Stone from the Sun'.

Like Handel, Hendrix was already fairly famous when he arrived in London but, again like Handel, it was his time in England that turned him into a genuine star: hits such as 'Hey Joe' and 'Purple Haze' meant that when he travelled back home to the United States he was a much bigger noise than when he had left it. In other words, London cannot quite claim to have made Jimi Hendrix but certainly it was his gigs at the likes of the Marquee and the Astoria, Brixton Road's Ram Jam Club and the Royal Albert Hall that nourished his reputation. (Let's not forget either that the other two members of the Jimi Hendrix Experience were both British, musicians who had already made their names tramping the London scene.)

In a way, and which many now take for granted, the guitarist's sudden death at just twenty-seven years old placed him among the immortals. It also qualified him for founder membership of the rock aristocracy's strangest club – sitting alongside Brian Jones, Janis Joplin, Jim Morrison, the Grateful Dead's 'Pigpen' McKernan and others, all of whom died at precisely the same young age. The circumstances of Hendrix's death remain controversial to this day, however. Officially, the greatest guitar player in history choked on vomit after taking nine sleeping pills – surprisingly there was no evidence of addiction to illegal drugs – and the coroner recorded an open verdict on a death certificate that was also, briefly, displayed at his old Mayfair address.

Chapter 2

SPITALFIELDS AND THE CITY

5. John Stow (c.1525-1605)

St Andrew Undershaft, St Mary Axe, EC3

Towards the end of his life Stow was said to be so poor that he was only half-joking when he sought business advice from beggars, and he was saved from utter penury only by an order from James I permitting him to solicit from 'amongst our loving subjects' voluntary contributions and 'kind gratuities'.

He was nevertheless one of the earliest and most celebrated chroniclers of London and his massively detailed *Survey of London* has rarely if ever been out of print (in more than four hundred years). He is also one of only a handful of individuals whose lives are officially commemorated in one of the small but colourful pieces of ceremonial that make up the City of London's annual calendar.

Each year the Lord Mayor of London, attended by other city officials and grandees, replaces a quill in the alabaster hand of Stow's effigy in the church of St Andrew Undershaft. The ceremony takes place on or near 5 April – the day of Stow's death – the church in question being the historian's parish church. (It is also a rare survivor of the Great Fire, the Blitz and in the 1990s several well-funded attacks on the Square Mile by Irish republicans.)

Stow was a Londoner of long descent, the son and grandson of a Cornhill tallow-chandler who though apprenticed to a merchant tailor developed a strong, life-long interest in historical and antiquarian matters. Working as a tailor for more than thirty years he was also responsible for a number of significant publications, starting in his mid-twenties with an expanded edition of Chaucer's verse, and with copies of his original *Survey* first offered for sale in 1598.

This, his masterwork, was possibly produced only as a diversion from his other labours but, like the diary of Samuel Pepys, his wide interests, a highly retentive memory and a skill for shaping a narrative imbued its two volumes with a vibrancy that makes the *Survey* a unique document of life in Tudor London. It was also helpful that its author enjoyed such a long life, so that towards the end of his time Stow was able, for example, to recall meeting in his youth individuals who could in turn remember the future Richard III when he was still just a 'comely prince'.

Like others writing about London before and since, much of the legwork for the volumes required Stow to explore individual city wards and parishes at length and on foot. Here an undoubted eye for detail was further supplemented by many hours spent researching old City of London records and documents, the antiquarian in Stow searching for the information needed to flesh out the evidence of his own eyes. Significantly these included many old monastic muniments, the precious contents of which might otherwise have been lost were it not for Stow's analysis and commentary.

This combination of what Stow himself described as 'many a weary mile's travel' and 'many a cold winter night's study' produced something quaint but still entertaining and hugely informative. The writing mixes fact with anecdote, and description with opinion, in a manner that a more serious scholar might have questioned. But in describing so many aspects of London life, Stow's *Survey* provides a genuinely unique record of the architecture of the walled city during the reign of Elizabeth I, as well as the living conditions of its people and many of its social customs.

AN EMPTY TOMB

The picture of Stow that emerges from his own writing and that of his biographers is of an attractive man, one who 'lived peacefully, and died of the stone collicke, being four score yeare of age'. He was buried in his parish church of St Andrew Undershaft, beneath a large memorial of Derbyshire marble and alabaster. Erected by his wife Elizabeth in 1605, and restored by the Merchant Taylors' Company three hundred years later, it shows him seated in his study, surrounded by his books and writing a manuscript. It is one of the most celebrated monuments in the City of London, but sadly there is no body beneath it. Having complained so bitterly during his lifetime at the way in which the bodies of the 'ancient dead' were thrown out to make room for others, Stow's grave was itself 'spoiled of his injured remains by certain men in the year 1732'. Both box and bones were discarded, and John Stow must be presumed to be lost forever.

That he covers so much ground in such minute and vivid detail means it is possible even now to follow his perambulations around the city, and to do so whilst hearing his voice describing what he can see. He complains about rising prices of everything from beef to soap, and new building developments – precisely the sort of stuff, in other words, which exercises Londoners today. The portrait he paints is one of a growing, successful and highly energetic city, a place where no sooner does one building come down than another goes up in its place. Like many Londoners today, he may not have liked much of what he saw and there is plenty of regret about what was being lost; but as many do today, he accepts change as the only constant and gets on with his life.

Notwithstanding the continuing penury of its author, the *Survey* must be adjudged a considerable commercial success, and indeed it was expanded and reissued within a very few years of its publication. Following Stow's death the process continued, and it was printed and reprinted on a regular basis, often edited, corrected and expanded by others who, as Stow might have done, could describe London as 'being birthplace and breeder to us'. Today, much like the diary of Samuel Pepys, it is the detail that makes it such an invaluable historical document and such a compelling read.

6. Sir Hiram S. Maxim
(1840-1916)

57d Hatton Garden, EC1

Profoundly deaf in later life as a direct result of his early experiments with things that go bang, Maxim's legacy is an especially deadly one. As he lay dying in south London in November 1916 so too did hundreds of thousands in northern France, the Battle of the Somme alone seeing more than one million young men cut down in the trenches by a myriad variations of the more-than-usually lethal weapon that bore his name.

American-born but resident in England for almost half his life, Maxim took British citizenship in 1900 and was knighted the following year. His machine wasn't the first – London lawyer James Puckle patented one as long ago as 1718[*] – but Maxim's was more efficient, much more deadly, and it soon conquered the world. He always claimed that his inspiration was a throwaway comment from an acquaintance, a suggestion that in pursuit of a fortune he should 'invent something that will enable these Europeans to cut each others' throats with greater facility'. The truth, however, was that he already had solid family connections with the arms business, and that both his father and brother were inventors specializing in military explosives.

Married twice – possibly bigamously – Maxim settled in West Norwood but it was in his workshop at Hatton Garden that he put into practice his brilliant concept for using the energy from a gun's recoil to reload and ready it to be fired again. Once perfected, the result was the

---

[*] Bizarrely this was designed to fire special bullets, square in section, intended specifically for killing and wounding Ottoman Turks.

MORE RIDING THAN FLYING

Aside from the gun that bears his name one of Maxim's most successful creations was his so-called Captive Flying Machine, an amusement park ride that he created primarily to fund his more serious work. It is credited with generating genuine public interest in powered flight – an area he personally found to be hugely exciting – although Maxim himself experienced a rare failure when attempting on his own account to build practical flying machines for public sale.

In an effort to get properly airborne he is thought to have made a substantial investment of more than £20,000 in the 1890s, all of it from his own funds. But in truth his dreams were running far ahead of technology and even the huge 110-foot wingspan Maxim envisaged for his new, pilotless aeroplane was not sufficient to offset the very considerable weight of the steam engines fitted either side of the fuselage. A 3.5 ton prototype was completed, and on its third attempt is said by some to have lifted a few feet above the ground. Unfortunately, when it crashed back down to earth it was badly damaged, and its creator lost interest in the idea from that point on.

world's first truly automatic weapon, a device capable of discharging a horrifying five hundred rounds per minute.

Bizarrely, various working prototypes of the gun were tested in the garden of the house at West Norwood, its creator thoughtfully placing announcements in local newspapers on firing days to remind neighbours to keep their windows open in order to avoid the danger of them being shattered by force of the blast. Carefully posed photographs from this period show the weapon in all its polished, brassy glory, the inventor proudly perched on its firing seat but looking decidedly out of place with his immaculate white beard and hair and in formal morning dress.

During his years in London Maxim patented several different versions of the gun – 'gas, recoil and blow-back' – each of which depended on a single automatic action to close the breech and to compress a spring thereby using the recoil energy from one shot to prepare the gun for the next one. By 1883 a working version was in full production and on sale, one of Maxim's earliest customers being the journalist and explorer Henry Morton Stanley, who took one with him on his expedition to find David Livingstone.

First seen in action in the Boer War, within less than a decade the Maxim gun was in service with both the British Army and the Royal Navy. In such hands it proved to be an invaluable asset, Britain possessing a large empire it needed to protect and still demonstrating a desire to expand. With demand rising, and the London workshop soon too small to cope, the Maxim Gun Company quickly relocated to Kent. Eventually it was to merge with Vickers, a large and successful armaments firm that survived until the tail end of the twentieth century.

It was the gun, of course, which made Maxim's name and his fortune, but as the aforementioned fairground ride suggests, Sir Hiram was a tireless and indefatigable inventor of much else besides. Above all he delighted in finding sound, commercial solutions to the problems that beset the public, and even as a teenager had built mousetraps able automatically to reset themselves. He managed to sell early versions to local mill owners, afterwards filing the first of more than 270 individual patents that would bear his name. (Sadly there is no evidence, referencing Ralph Waldo Emerson, that the world ever beat a path to his door as a consequence; but then the United States Patent and Trademark Office is known to have nearly 4,500 designs on its books for improved mousetraps of this kind.)

Maxim's other inventions included an electric light bulb with a carbon filament – making him one of nearly two dozen inventors whose designs predate those of Thomas Edison – as well as an electric pressure regulator, which won him the first of many international awards, the French Legion d'honneur. In his London workshop he also created a more efficient type of gun cartridge, one that used a new smokeless powder called cordite, enabling a concealed soldier to fire at an enemy without giving away his position.

In the final analysis the Wright Brothers beat him into the air, and Edison definitely stole his thunder with a better light bulb. But even with just the gun to his name one cannot readily deny that Maxim served his adopted country well, and with it the great British Empire. The slaughter of the Somme was still years away and would be horrific, but a knighthood seemed assured. Towards the end of Queen Victoria's reign she agreed that the American-born pioneer should have one, and when she died before it could be conferred it was left to Edward VII to do the honours.

7. George Fabian Lawrence
(1862–1939)

30–32 Cheapside, City of London, EC2

Known to all as 'Stony Jack', the asthmatic Lawrence was a pawnbroker as well as an antiquities dealer and collector based in south London. He rose to prominence for his shady if reasonably well-intentioned role in the quiet transfer of a priceless collection of sixteenth- and seventeenth-century jewels to what is now the Museum of London.

Deriving its name from one of the principal thoroughfares of the Square Mile, the Cheapside Hoard was uncovered by workmen engaged in demolishing a small cluster of decayed properties that formed part of London's medieval Goldsmith's Row. The find, conceivably the most important from London's soil in two thousand years, was made in the summer of 1912 when navvies working at the site stumbled upon a veritable Aladdin's cave of treasure.

Strictly speaking, the more than four hundred pieces of Elizabethan and Jacobean jewellery should have been handed straight to the Worshipful Company of Goldsmiths. As freeholder, the liverymen had inserted a clause in the demolition agreement requiring exactly this of 'any antiquities and articles and objects of interest or value'.

Nothing of the sort happened. Stony Jack was already a well-known figure in dark corners of the city and would frequently loiter at demolition sites chatting to the workmen, having long ago let it be known that he could be helpful to them. He was, as one put it, 'the bloke at Wandsworth who buys old stones and bits of pottery … he's a good sport. If you dig up an old pot or a coin and take it to him he'll tell you what it is and buy it off you.' Crucially, even if the object in question was rubbish, Stony Jack would still stump up the price of a half pint of beer.

He knew the navvies well and the navvies knew him, and every few days he could be spotted on a building site or round the corner in a pub transacting a little business over a glass or two. Little wonder, then, that when the men hit the jackpot – 'we've struck a toy shop, I thinks guv'nor', is how one of them put it – their first thought was to call in on Lawrence.

To his credit his first thought was of the new London Museum, which was soon to open in St James's. In great secrecy it was arranged for the haul to be removed to the home of one of the trustees. At his house in Berkeley Square Lewis Victor Harcourt MP – Loulou to his chums, and later the 1st Viscount Harcourt – instructed Lawrence to pay off the navvies and to secure the collection as quietly as possible. For this Stony Jack was to be made Inspector of Excavations, a new and prestigious post presumably cooked up on the spot.

Among the first of very few visitors allowed to see the hoard were the king and queen. Then, with almost indecent haste, it was agreed that the collection should be donated to the museum, with Harcourt named as the donor. No consideration was given to the Goldsmiths and their contract, nor was an inquest ever held into the jewels' provenance, which ordinarily would have seen them transferred to the rival British Museum. (This assumes, as one must, that the Cheapside Hoard would have been declared treasure trove.)

That a certain amount of skulduggery was involved there is no doubt, and not just on the part of Stony Jack. He gained instant respectability from his new role and a certain amount of cash after selling a piece (that he had somehow been allowed to keep) to the Victoria and Albert Museum. Harcourt, meanwhile, gained the glory due to a big benefactor, and perhaps that peerage too. And, of course, the navvies got their free beer. But by far the biggest winner was the Museum of London – a later amalgamation of the London and Guildhall museums – and for that, more than a hundred years later, we still have Stony Jack to thank.

8. Polly the Parrot (1884–1926)

Wine Office Court, Fleet Street, EC4

At the nascent British Broadcasting Corporation, 1926 has gone down in history as the year that the dour Lord Reith issued his famous edict requiring newsreaders to wear dinner jackets even though they were appearing on the wireless. Someone high up at the BBC must have had something of a sense of humour even then, however, for it was also the year that its service broadcast the obituary of a mere parrot.

Eventually stuffed and mounted in a glass case displayed in the ground floor tap room of one of London's most historic old taverns, the bird was notorious for entertaining visitors to the bar at Ye Olde Cheshire Cheese.

Despite the name, Polly was actually a cock bird, and for four decades he was one of the pub's most celebrated characters – no mean feat in a place where the roster of drinkers over the years included the likes of Charles Dickens, Oliver Goldsmith, Mark Twain, Alfred Lord Tennyson, G.K. Chesterton and Sir Arthur Conan Doyle.

Samuel Johnson was almost certainly another regular – not least, perhaps, as of his seventeen London addresses the only one still standing is just around the corner in Gough Square. Rather disappointingly there is no documentary evidence for this, but Johnson liked pubs, this one was his local, and it has long been popular with hacks. That said, it is wholly unlikely that the doctor

LONDON'S MIGHTIEST PUDDING

Regulars even now call Polly's old haunt 'the House' and it is still a popular place for lunch among those working in the area, although sadly the bill of fare no longer features the savoury suet pudding for which it was once famous. According to nineteenth-century sources each one had a cooked weight in excess of fifty pounds, took nearly a day and a night to boil, and had 'entombed therein beefsteaks, kidneys, oysters, larks, mushrooms and wondrous spices and gravies, the secret of which is known only to the compounder'. It was said at the time that the aroma on a breezy day reached as far as the Stock Exchange.

sat in here consuming ale and biscuits whilst mulling over particularly tricky definitions for his famous dictionary, although the myth that he did has proved an enduring one and is an attractive image to ponder whilst in one of the pub's several pleasantly gloomy panelled rooms.

The pub itself is one of London's oldest, dating from just after the Great Fire although the underpinnings are far older than this and the cellars are thought once to have been part of a thirteenth-century Carmelite monastery. An early, pre-Great Fire landlord was Thomas Cheshire, hence the pub's name, and it was one of his successors who introduced Polly to the place in the 1880s. Much of Polly's appeal depended on his very considerable vocabulary, a lot of it decidedly blue in tone. Besides impersonating customers, the bird's chief party trick was to imitate the sound of a champagne cork being drawn from a bottle.

This last attribute most famously came into its own in November 1918. As Londoners celebrated the armistice, legend has it that Polly almost expired after heroically mimicking no fewer than four hundred times the sound of a cork popping. With Fleet Street's finest there to witness this extraordinary achievement, Polly's reputation as one of London's great eccentrics was thus assured. His death, when it came eight years later, was marked not only by Lord Reith's po-faced BBC but in obituaries in more than two hundred newspapers across the English-speaking world.

9. David Rodinsky (1925-69)

19 Princelet Street, E1

Was he tall, short, educated, uneducated, well-heeled or on his uppers, a rare and insightful scholar or maybe just simple-minded? Not much is known with any certainty about David Rodinsky, aside from the fact that he lived in a cluttered garret above an old synagogue in London's East End – and that then, suddenly, he didn't.

The subject of an unusual and fascinating book by artist Rachel Lichtenstein and psychogeographer Iain Sinclair (*Rodinsky's Room*, published 1999), in 1969 the middle-aged Rodinsky seemed to disappear without a trace. For more than ten years the attic room he had occupied remained locked and undisturbed – his books, maps and papers lying haphazardly on every surface together with scrappy disconnected notes, many of which were scrawled in obscure and moribund languages. It was even said, by one of the witnesses to the moment when the chaotic time capsule was finally breached in 1980, that an impression left by Rodinsky's head was still visible on the pillow of the unmade single bed.

As mysterious in his way as Kaspar Hauser or D.B.

Cooper, the bare facts might not alone have turned Rodinsky into legend or enabled him to become part of East End folklore. He was nevertheless co-opted into the area's modern mythology, much like Jack the Ripper had been many decades earlier and, later, the Krays. It helped that there were witnesses willing to share their own fragmentary memories of the disappeared man, but it was abundantly clear, however, that no one in the neighbourhood was even close to assembling these into the story of a life.

Lichtenstein set out to do this, and over many months she was able to do so although the story that emerged was far from happy and poses almost as many questions as it answers. Like many in this very fluid part of London, Rodinsky was born into a family of refugees, in this case from Ukraine. His was an Orthodox family who moved into an area that over hundreds of years had absorbed communities of Protestants from France and Muslims from the Indian subcontinent as well as tens of thousands of Jews from the Russian Empire. By the time of Rodinsky's birth (in 1925) the latter grouping accounted for more than 90 per cent of the local population, many of them crammed into the once elegant former homes of Huguenot weavers – tall, narrow townhouses that had been divided and subdivided as the population swelled.

Like the Huguenots before them, this new immigrant community gradually prospered through a combination of hard work, entrepreneurship and education. Eventually its members moved on, many relocating to what became known as the Beigel Belt suburbs of north-west London and assimilating to a degree which enabled them to fit in whilst retaining a clear and important sense of identity. Not everyone was so fortunate, however, and Rodinsky found himself among the stragglers. His own family perhaps never reconciled itself to its dislocation and forced resettlement, and both Rodinsky and a sibling spent time in psychiatric institutions on London's suburban fringe.

Eventually it emerged that Rodinsky didn't simply disappear in 1969, he died. Aged only forty-four, alone and probably unknown in a Surrey psychiatric home, he was afterwards buried as a pauper in a grave on a windswept site just off the M25. With no one to mourn him David Rodinsky's story might have ended there, had the upstairs room been cleared out and his possessions disposed of once it was apparent that he would not be returning.

The fact that they weren't is what gives the tale its considerable appeal, and their discovery years later makes the unusual genuinely extraordinary. That has not prevented cynics arguing that it is only the two authors' passion and their artistry that have turned Rodinsky's life into a legend, or that the process was assisted by a fascinated media that leapt on the almost *Marie Celeste*-like quality of the narrative. But of course much the same could be said of the Krays, who were after all only criminals, or even of Jack the Ripper, who was neither London's most gruesome killer nor by any means its most prolific.

10. 'Adam' (c.1996–2001)

Tower Bridge, EC3

Around fifty bodies each year are pulled from the River Thames, of which approximately four-fifths are suicides, most of which result from jumping off a bridge. Most occur during the winter months, with a peak around Christmas, and in summer the occasional drunk jumps in without considering the consequences. The rest are assumed to have been murdered.

The unenviable task of recovering the bodies falls to the Marine Support Unit, the old Thames Division with its mortuary facility at Wapping Police Station. Those found are held for identification in a tank covered by a blue tarpaulin, which is visible from passing pleasure boats. Each one is labelled DB1, DB2, etc. – shorthand for Dead Body, with the numbers being reset to one each New Year's Day.

Occasionally officers choose something slightly more personal, however, as was the case with the torso found floating close to Tower Bridge on 21 September 2001. It belonged to a little boy thought to have been five or six years old when he died and, suspecting that his death had some ritualistic element to it, the police investigating the case named him 'Adam'.

Adam's remains, spotted by a pedestrian on the bridge, were floating upstream in the direction of Tate Modern and the Globe Theatre, and are thought to have been in the water for up to ten days. This in itself is not unusual: it can frequently take two to three weeks for a body to be recovered, by which time it can be in a dreadful state not least because, as a river policeman once put it, 'the water is very cruel, the river is tidal, you get hit by boats and barges and attacked by seabirds'.

The grim discovery of Adam – together with a quantity of half-burned candles on the foreshore, wrapped in cloth bearing a common African name, Adekoyejo Fola Adeoye – led to stories in the press of ritual murder and 'voodoo killings'. Pollen in the victim's lungs indicated that he had been in London for at least seventy-two hours, but the suspicion was that he had been brought here expressly to be killed. Toxicology reports also showed that he had been alive but paralysed at the moment when his throat was cut.

When the torso was pulled from the water it was dressed only in a pair of orange shorts, of a type sold by Woolworths in Germany and Austria. Nothing else about Adam's identity could be determined with any certainty. Mineral and vegetable matter found in his stomach included minute particles of bone and of gold, suggesting that Adam had been a victim of the sort of 'Muti' killing known to take place in many parts of sub-Saharan Africa. Later pioneering work on radio isotopes found in all human bone narrowed it down by providing a link to the geology of a particular area of south-west Nigeria close to Benin City and Ibadan.

Such ritualized murders are usually carried out in the belief that the bodies of particular children are sacred, the remains frequently being disposed of in flowing water. Thereafter certain body parts command huge sums for use in primitive rituals and medicines, and are said to bring good luck, sexual virility and success in business. Rare in Africa, and never before seen in England, a couple of similar killings had, according to newspaper reports, recently come to light in Germany and Belgium.

In 2003 police working on Adam's case announced that they had arrested twenty-one people in raids on nine London addresses involving more than two hundred officers. Most of the ten men and eleven women were arrested for immigration offences, identity fraud and passport forgery, but the BBC reported the discovery of a number of items that, according to the Met's Commander Andy Baker, 'would raise a few eyebrows. They look like some element of ritualism is involved.'

Another suspect was subsequently jailed for child trafficking but no charges specific to the torso followed the raids, and after a further three years of investigations the police seemed to have drawn a blank. Adam was finally laid to rest in an unmarked grave somewhere in London. A police spokesperson told the BBC it was 'a sad, thoughtful and dignified service to celebrate Adam's short life', which was attended only by those closely involved in the case.

A decade on, the police still had little more to report, beyond the hope that the enormous publicity surrounding the case would dissuade others from attempting something similar. Then, in late 2012, detectives involved in the case described as a major breakthrough the news that an apparently reliable witness could identify the torso as belonging to a child called Patrick Erhabor. A retired police chief inspector who had worked on the original investigation told the *Daily Mail* that 'without a name murders are very hard to solve. This is a crucial starting point for us and it should lead us to who killed him.' Even so, nearly three years later, the case was still unsolved.

Chapter 3

WESTMINSTER AND WHITEHALL

11. John St John Long
(1798–1834)

84 Harley Street, W1

Though considered utterly respectable in more recent times, at least until the bill is presented, London's medical quarter in and around Harley Street built much of its reputation on unorthodox practices, snake oil and quackery.

John St John Long was a charlatan with no medical training who nevertheless managed to build a client base that wholeheartedly subscribed to several weird experimental techniques intended to prolong their lives – or at least to relieve them of cash. A man who dabbled in the world of arts as well as science, Long was widely known in both fields for his somewhat outrageous assessments of his own talents. Thus, while studying anatomy, he promoted himself as a painter of historical subjects, even going so far as to send several works to the Tate Gallery, although it should be noted that these have spent far more time in storage than on display.

Artistically his high point was probably a vast nine-foot canvas called *The Temptation in the Wilderness*, unveiled in 1825, but perhaps unimpressed with the reception given to this allegorical scene he shortly afterwards set his sights on establishing himself as a doctor on Harley Street.

His specialism of choice was the treatment of consumption (or TB, tuberculosis). His cure involved locating a site from which the disease could 'escape' the confines of the body. On the highly questionable assumption that a disease required only such an exit point for the patient to be cured, Long's intention was to create large wounds on his patients' persons, telling them that the inevitable and invariably painful discharges carried with them the consumption.

This unorthodox treatment gained unfortunate publicity for Long when a young patient died. Sixteen-year-old Miss Cashin was a member of a respectable and wealthy family, and Long duly set about her with a knife. As the wound grew in size the patient weakened and, when subjected to questions from her understandably distressed relations, Long laughed off their fears as the unnecessary worries of the ignorant.

Miss Cashin nevertheless became sicker and sicker, as her vitality drained through the open wound. Long prescribed a glass of port. When this didn't work, another – legitimate – surgeon was called for to give a second opinion. Unfortunately Mr Brodie arrived too late from Savile Row, and the girl died.

A coroner's inquest was ordered and following an examination of the body it was determined that in fact no one could have survived the effects of Long's wounding. At this stage no one questioned the theory of the treatment, only the practice, and after three hours in the jury room a guilty verdict saw Long fined £250 on a charge of manslaughter. For Long, as a wealthy Harley Street practitioner, the money was neither here nor there. The debt was quickly paid and, released from custody, he returned to his practice later the same day.

Fortunately a higher form of justice soon intervened; John St John Long was destined to die aged just thirty-six. The cause? Consumption. The cure? One that its inventor decided not to risk.

12. Jack Black
(nineteenth century, dates unknown)

Buckingham Palace, SW1

The old London adage that 'one is never more than six feet away from a rat' has most likely been around almost as long as the rat and even now it is estimated that four thousand rats are born in the city every hour.

The problem of vermin of all kinds is a long-standing one and, in this vein, records from George III's reign show a number of less than prestigious appointments to the royal household. These include a 'mole-taker' and a bug exterminator, with Andrew Cook of Holborn claiming to 'have cured 16,000 beds with great applause' including several within the royal palaces. Such individuals were never granted the same right as luxury goods makers to describe themselves as 'By Appointment', but they must have been kept busy and, as such, come to number among the regular suppliers to the royal household.

Buckingham Palace has certainly relied on the services of a rat catcher, and in Queen Victoria's day the job fell to Jack Black. He is said to have cut quite a dash in his self-made uniform of green topcoat, scarlet waistcoat and white leather breeches, and in Henry Mayhew's *London Labour and the London Poor* he described Black as wearing a huge leather belt inset with cast iron rats.

Mayhew goes into great detail about the pitfalls of the job, and it sounds grim. By Black's own account the job of rat catching had him nearly dead three times and his skin was a mass of bite scars and boils as large as fish eyes. The latter he had to lance himself, a glass or two of stout providing both Dutch courage and a measure of local anaesthetic.

Handling the rats was even so a natural thing for Black, a skill he claimed to have acquired at the age of nine. As a self-professed master of the art in later life, he went on to offer his services to the general public as well as royalty. Mayhew describes one incident that saw Black extract no fewer than three hundred of the creatures from a single hole at the home of Mrs Brown, the rats as at home in a slum as they were with a sovereign and clearly no respecters of class or status.

13. Sir Henry Morton Stanley
(1841-1904)

6 Richmond Terrace, SW1

Arguably as famous an utterance as any in two thousand years of human history, Stanley's 'Dr Livingstone,

I presume?' may be entirely apocryphal yet the phrase entered the language almost immediately. It is also just about the only thing many people know or think they know about this restless and energetic Welshman, who in later life became the MP for Lambeth North.

Born to an unmarried mother, and spending his formative years in a Denbighshire workhouse, John Rowlands escaped to the United States at the earliest opportunity. Changing his name on arrival, and adopting an American accent, he enlisted in both the Confederate and Union armies during the civil war, and later the Union Navy before jumping ship and becoming a journalist.

Success in this latter endeavour came early. Stanley's engagingly direct writing style and his fearless sense of adventure made him the ideal foreign correspondent, and in 1869 James Gordon Bennett Jr, proprietor of the *New York Herald*, sent him to the much storied 'dark continent'. His task was to find the missing missionary and explorer David Livingstone, from whom nothing had been heard for some time.

The expedition, which took nearly two years to organize, was going to be dangerous. It was also spectacularly well funded, with more than two hundred native bearers engaged for the seven hundred mile trek through the infested African forest. For Stanley it held out the promise of worldwide fame if Livingstone could be run

A FAMOUS PHRASE,
BUT DID HE EVEN SAY IT?

Precisely what occurred at Lake Tanganyika will never be known as Stanley destroyed the relevant pages in his journal. Many fellow explorers remained dismissive of his talents, including Sir Richard Burton who described him shooting tribesmen 'as if they were monkeys'. Such accounts have been disputed, however, as has the story that he cut off his dog's tail, cooked it and fed it back to the poor animal. Stanley remains a hugely divisive figure even so — controversial enough for the government of the day officially to suppress many details of his adventures — and it was not until 2011 that the town of Denbigh finally erected a statue in honour of its most famous son.

to ground, a significant consideration for someone who throughout his life remained haunted by his humble, illegitimate beginnings.

In the event it took him eight months to find his man, and Stanley's version of the encounter did indeed make celebrities of them both when it was splashed across the press.

Much of the tarnish on Stanley's reputation relates to his close involvement with the King of the Belgians, in particular Leopold II's desire to subjugate vast areas of the Congo for his own enrichment. Stanley had explored the territory and shared the king's dream of bringing it under European rule; unable to get British backing he allied himself to Leopold.

With terrible efficiency the pair set out to enslave and brutalize the entire population, the creation of the Congo Free State – as Leopold's personal possession rather than as a Belgian colony – remaining the single worst chapter in nineteenth-century colonial history. Novelist Joseph Conrad described it as 'the vilest scramble for loot that ever disfigured the history of human conscience' – and Stanley's reputation will likely never recover for his part in the death of as many as ten million Congolese men, women and children.

By 1890 he was back in Europe, however, and from his home just off Whitehall he embarked on a series of hugely popular lecture tours based on such bestselling books as *Through the Dark Continent, In Darkest Africa* and, of course, *How I Found Livingstone.* When it came to the Congo, little if any mention was made of the worst excesses: slaves' hands were routinely amputated as punishment, and at least one captain made a collection of Africans' heads. But the public was eager to hear stories of action and derring-do, and Stanley had plenty of them and the talent to bring them alive.

By this time a British subject once more, and married to the painter Dorothy Tennant, Stanley was elected as Liberal Unionist member for Lambeth in 1895. As such a popular and well-known figure he held the seat for five

years, during which time he was made a Knight Grand
Cross of the Most Honourable Order of the Bath.

As Sir Henry Morton Stanley GCB MP he might thus
be said at last to have banished the taint of his low, illegitimate birth; but the truth is that he made no impression
whatever as a parliamentarian. Personally he admitted
that he was simply too old to exchange his 'open-air
habits for the asphyxiating atmosphere of the House of
Commons'. But more likely is that, in his declining years,
a great adventurer was manoeuvred into a grotesquely
unsuitable role by his wife and mother-in-law.

For years the former had refused to allow him to
return to the Africa he loved, while the latter – something
of a battle-axe, and the owner of the house on Richmond
Terrace – clearly enjoyed the prestige of having a tame MP
in the family. Henry, in other words – known throughout
Africa as *Bula Matari*, 'the breaker of rocks' – was actually
just another henpecked husband.

14. 'Lawrence of Arabia' (1888-1935)

14 Barton Street, SW1

Combining a talent for self-publicity with a pathological
desire for privacy, it is perhaps unsurprising that Colonel

Thomas Edward Lawrence remains one of the more mysterious and enigmatic figures of the twentieth century.

His adventures in the Middle East are legendary, at least in the cinematic version with its numerous historical inaccuracies. His sudden, violent death riding his Brough Superior along a lane in Dorset has similarly helped to make this particular marque *the* most sought after and most expensive motorcycle in the world. But that he spent time in London is less well known, although his brief and irregular sojourns in Westminster were very important both to Lawrence himself and to the development of the mythology that has long surrounded him.

For some years this neat Georgian townhouse on Barton Street was leased by the architect Sir Herbert Baker, whose commissions included important rebuilding work at nearby Westminster Abbey as well as much of New Delhi and a stand at Lord's.* Friendly with Lawrence at Oxford, Baker offered him the use of the attic in the early 1920s, at a time when the former soldier and diplomat was employed at the Colonial Office as political adviser to Winston Churchill.

Baker's garret looked like the perfect hiding place from journalists and others who were keen to make something of Lawrence's wartime exploits fomenting the

---

* Unfortunately the same hand was also responsible for demolishing Sir John Soane's Bank of England, a move described by the architectural historian Nikolaus Pevsner as the City of London's 'greatest architectural crime ... of the 20th century'.

'PHYSICALLY SMALL, WITH A HEAD DISPROPORTIONATELY LARGE'

The worldwide success of David Lean's 1962 epic *Lawrence of Arabia*, and long-limbed Peter O'Toole's dashing performance in the lead role, effectively reset the template for how most now view the man himself.

In reality Lawrence was brooding and short – less than five foot six inches – and suffered a number of physical setbacks, beginning with a broken leg as a teenager, which never afterwards grew. Frequently beset by boils and malaria, he broke a collarbone during a 'plane crash in 1919 on a flight from London to Cairo – it was a bad one in which both pilots were killed – and in all sustained more than sixty different wounds during his Middle East service and later military career.

Arab Revolt against Turkish Ottoman rule. As a refuge from all this it was ideal, 'the best-and-freest place I ever lived in', Lawrence called it, clearly delighting in the fact that no one discovered him there, although plenty tried. In this he was helped by a lifestyle that was ascetic and more or less nocturnal, Lawrence refusing 'all food, fire or hot water' and those working down below in the architect's office claiming never to have heard a sound from upstairs.

Lawrence, however, was anything but idle during his time hiding away in Barton Street and indeed No. 14 – somewhat paradoxically – was to be the place where the self-styled hermit cemented his celebrity by completing the final draft of *The Seven Pillars of Wisdom*. This immense and colourful exercise in autohagiography could not fail to raise his public profile to the rafters, and in the year following it was to provide nearly all the material for the myths and legends that dogged him for the rest of his life.

Purportedly unhappy with the effects of his celebrity status Lawrence twice changed his name – to Aircraftman Ross, then Private Shaw – joining the RAF incognito (he was recruited by Captain W.E. Johns of *Biggles* fame) and then the army before asking to be returned once more to the RAF. He also abandoned Barton Street for a hut in Epping Forest, before finally recognizing that – in large part due to his own published version of his life – his face was now simply too well known for him to hide away for very long.

The obvious question is: how seriously should we take his desire to be left alone? The first quarter of a million words of the book were lost by Lawrence while changing trains at Reading, and a second, even longer version, he let people know he had burned. Thereafter he worked hard for years to see the work through to publication, producing no fewer than four different versions of a document so manifestly self-promoting that it is hard to credit any subsequent claims that he preferred anonymity. His removal to Epping Forest is equally suspicious, an escape to a location hardly remote from London especially as he chose the popular, much visited beauty spot of Pole Hill as the place to erect his hut.

That Lawrence had talent and great physical courage has never been in doubt. He also had more than his fair share of bizarre quirks, for example displaying a genuine dislike of being touched by anyone, yet inviting friends to beat him on the buttocks. Clearly his was a complex contradictory character, but for all his protestations of modesty and self-doubt he was nevertheless a relentless self-promoter and a highly skilled showman.

While attempting to bury himself in the anonymity of the 'other ranks' he continued to seek and value the company of eminent men such as Churchill, Edward Elgar and George Bernard Shaw (with whom he corresponded at length). Clouds Hill, the tiny cottage he rented in Dorset, was likewise kept devoid of all comforts, yet weekends and holidays saw Lawrence welcomed by the great and good into many of England's grandest country houses.

Indeed even Lawrence's favoured mode of transport was exceptional, his Brough Superior being decidedly out of the ordinary. Advertised as the 'Rolls-Royce of motorcycles', apparently with the consent of Sir Henry Royce (at least up until the moment its creator, George Brough, attempted to build a car of his own), it was the finest such machine of its day. Lawrence bought eight of them in succession, each of which would have cost around £150 at a time when his fellow aircraftmen would have been earning just a pound or two per week. Clouds Hill indeed might have been bought for less, but T.E. Lawrence wasn't going to catch the bus for anyone.

Observing such behaviour the composer and diplomat Lord Berners famously accused the war hero of 'always backing into the limelight' – and not for the first time he got him in one.

15. Lord Reith (1889-1971)

6 Barton Street, SW1

Living around the corner from T.E. Lawrence, and his near contemporary, John Reith's name is still the one most closely associated in the public's mind with the formation and administration of the world's most famous public broadcaster.

Even now, after more than ninety years and in a multichannel universe, it is impossible to imagine daily life without the BBC, and almost as hard to imagine the BBC without Lord Reith.* In its earliest days the broadcaster

* This has a longer history than one might imagine and London played a leading role when Britain's first ever pay-TV channel – Greenwich Cablevision – made its first broadcast as long ago as July 1972 from a studio in Plumstead.

was a surprisingly small operation, with a staff of just four offering radio only. Then, as now, funding came from an annual licence fee, which in those days was ten shillings (fifty pence) payable by anyone with a wireless receiver. Reith joined as general manager within a month of the first broadcast in November 1922, arriving from Scotland with an engineering apprenticeship and after a short spell working for the Conservative Party.

Nothing in his background qualified him for running a broadcasting service, and years later Reith admitted that from the start he found himself confronting 'problems of which I had no experience: copyright and performing rights; Marconi patents; associations of concert artists, authors, playwrights, composers, music publishers, theatre managers, wireless manufacturers'.

At this time the British Broadcasting Company was still a private firm owned by a consortium of equipment manufacturers. As it developed, and its influence grew, Reith conceived a more exciting future for it as a *corporation* under independent, public ownership.

This view strengthened when the company came under very heavy pressure, as the only national broadcaster, from a number of vested interests during the General Strike of 1926. These included Downing Street, the striking unions and even the Church of England, but Reith soon had his way. The following year a new British Broadcasting Corporation was created under a

Royal Charter (and, it should be noted, in the teeth of considerable government opposition).

Perhaps having experienced so much external interference, Reith as the founding director general quickly adopted an autocratic, almost dictatorial approach to management. It was a style that would raise eyebrows today, and much of it might be considered unacceptable. But as with Frank Pick, the equally inspired chief executive at London Underground, his instincts as boss were good and his energy and commitment total.* Most significantly, and long before organizations began issuing what we now know as mission statements, it was Reith who set out a guiding philosophy, a decree that the BBC should above all seek to educate, inform and entertain. This is something it still strives to do today, and which many broadcasters around the world attempt to copy.

Even so, as the youngest of seven children of a United Free Church of Scotland minister, Lord Reith and his time at the helm are not without their comic aspects. Like the former prime minister Gordon Brown, one of those Scotsmen for whom the word 'dour' might have been coined, he famously insisted that newsreaders dress

---

* Interestingly, both men crossed swords with Winston Churchill and lost. Reith relinquished his post as the wartime Minister of Information immediately that Chamberlain stepped down, and Pick was shortly afterwards fired from the Ministry after questioning its role in producing propaganda.

in black tie even for radio broadcasts, and was rumoured to have refused to consider a presenter for a religious programme after the man in question was caught giving a female colleague an innocent peck on the cheek.

In fact there is no reliable evidence for this last story, although Reith certainly worked hard to instil higher standards of moral behaviour in his own employees as well as in the listening public. On Sunday mornings, for example, there were no broadcasts on the grounds that listeners were mostly in church – or should be. BBC staff were also liable to be sacked following divorces, and in 1929 when one of his news editors turned out to be the other man in Evelyn Waugh's marital breakdown it caused Reith considerable personal embarrassment. Returning to Broadcasting House to give an interview more than thirty years later, he was reportedly dismayed to find that builders working there had some topless pin-ups on display. In the interview itself he also admitted he had stopped watching television and listening to the radio after no longer being employed to do so.

Today, however, none of this quaint posturing and fogeyism comes to mind (nor should it) when one hears the word 'Reithian'. Instead, as a term, it is suggestive of the highest standards of public service, also a recognition that – notwithstanding his lordship's personal stiffness and hypocrisy (he is known to have had at least one office affair) – viewers and listeners alike owe a lot to John

Charles Walsham Reith. It was he who first promoted the idea of a national broadcaster's responsibility for educating and informing the public. It was also he who insisted this be achieved in a fair and equitable manner, and one that did not seek to attract the largest possible audience at the expense of a programme's artistic merit, impartiality or educative value.

Admittedly, maintaining this balance can be hard, harder certainly than it is to throw up one's arms or to point the finger every time the BBC appears briefly to fall short of its own relatively high standards. No licence fee payer likes everything that the BBC puts out – and the suspicion is that neither would Lord Reith. But just as it is hard to imagine our lives without it, it is harder still to imagine that without John Reith's example – and the long shadow that he casts – the BBC would have survived this long, or maintained a global reputation that even now no other broadcaster can match.

16. Margaret Thatcher (1925–2013)

10 Downing Street, SW1

A resident of London for more than half a century, at various times the MP for Finchley had homes in Dulwich,

Chelsea and Belgravia but the obvious association is still very much with 10 Downing Street.

This is not simply because she was Britain's first ever woman prime minister, nor even because she held office for longer than any other UK prime minister in the twentieth century, although the latter certainly goes some way towards explaining why even now she is more closely associated with No. 10 than most other PMs. Mostly it is because Lady Thatcher really loved the place (a surprisingly high number of her predecessors wouldn't even live there) and understood perfectly what she described as the 'sense of continuity and dignified authority that gives No. 10 its very special place in our national life'.

It is fitting, then, that Thatcher now has her own very special place inside No. 10. By this one is not referring to the prime ministerial portrait on the staircase, which they all get on their departure, from Sir Robert Walpole to Gordon Brown. Rather it is a charming figure of a straw-carrying thatcher situated above a door in one of the state rooms, a unique tribute to a serving PM, which was carved into the plasterwork when the Terracotta Dining Room was given its splendidly ornate gilded ceiling in 1989 by the architect Quinlan Terry.

'WE'LL NOT SEE HER LIKE AGAIN THIS LIFETIME'

Still a highly divisive figure in the way that decisive leaders always are, the convention is to say that Margaret Hilda Thatcher was admired and disliked in equal measure. In fact the electoral record during her time suggests otherwise, and she was by far the most popular politician of her generation. As for the hullabaloo that followed her death in 2013, it might be noted that as many tens of thousands lined the streets of London to pay their respects, only a few handfuls came to jeer and boo.

In a man's world her rise had been meteoric. Of modest middling origins, the Oxford-educated grocer's daughter made a very early start in politics, first standing for Parliament in her mid-twenties: by thirty-four she had secured the safe north London seat of Finchley. Appointed a minister in Edward Heath's government, she soon replaced him as Conservative leader before going on to chalk up three resounding election victories in 1979, 1983 and 1987.

That said, if the maxim is true that political careers always end in failure then her ignominious exit from No. 10 is as good a proof as any. With the Conservatives seemingly in meltdown by 1990, and perhaps not realizing the degree to which support for her personally had leached away within the party, she put her leadership on the line and then resigned in shock when the results failed to measure up. But while she was out, it was still to be another seven years before Labour got in.

Ahead of this, however, and for nearly twelve years, the Iron Lady was to exert a powerful influence – over her Cabinet and her party, over Parliament, and over Britain. (Also over the wider world, that very term – Iron Lady – having been coined by the Soviets not by the miners.) She was, in short, a phenomenon, an important and effective challenge to the existing order – again, not simply because she was a woman – and a whirlwind of change in a Britain where even the vaunted, bestselling Mini was being built at a loss and where incomes were taxed at up to 83 per cent – and 98 per cent if it was deemed 'unearned'.

Above all, Margaret Thatcher was determined to reduce state interference in people's lives, to rein in the power and influence of militant trades unions, and to cut public expenditure and the country's spiralling deficit. To this end, she worked hard to reverse the economic trend that was resoundingly downward, and to do something about Britain's near-necrotic nationalized industries.

The results were impressive and have proved long-lasting, and more than twenty-five years later it is significant that no other party has made any serious attempt to undo her work. But, inevitably, such radical surgery also left scars, and it is significant too that in parts of

Britain's former industrial heartland her name alone is still enough to start a fight.

Besides getting things done she was a formidable performer, and long before the term 'soundbite' became widely known she was recognized as a quotable source for the press. As early as 1965 she was telling voters, 'If you want something said, ask a man. If you want something done, ask a woman.' Her policies were just as down to earth, and she always insisted that they were 'based not on some economics theory, but on things I and millions like me were brought up with: an honest day's work for an honest day's pay; live within your means; put by a nest egg for a rainy day; pay your bills on time [and] support the police'.

Inevitably, some of the scripted witticisms sounded laboured, but probably no more than is normal among politicians. And even if she wasn't joking when she said she was 'extraordinarily patient, provided I get my own way in the end' Lady Thatcher was sufficiently candid to tell an audience, post-retirement in 2001, that 'on my way here I passed a local cinema and it turns out you were expecting me after all. The billboards read *The Mummy Returns*'.

In fact this particular joke was quite a good one, making light of the left's view of her as something out of a horror movie, one of the undead. In one sense, of course, they had a point: post-retirement, even post-*mortem* Lady

Thatcher does indeed live on and she does so in the way that only a genuinely historically significant figure can.

With the obvious but sole exception of Winston Churchill, her legacy is one that remains unmatched by any British political figure of the last hundred years or more. And in truth that's what the grumblers and mumblers really can't abide. Not what she did or what she stood for, but the fact that for a party which likes its heroes she is the real deal – something Labour conspicuously lacks, at least without going back many, many years.

Chapter 4

SOHO

17. 'Canaletto' (1697-1768)

41 Beak Street, W1

In much the same way that port became known as the Englishman's wine – from the seventeenth century onwards it was fortified on arrival in England, and much more of it was consumed here than ever it was in Portugal – it is hard to overstate the important role of the English and English patrons to the life of Giovanni Antonio Canal and the development of his art.

A talented painter of landscapes or *vedute*, most famously of Venice, Canaletto from the start found a ready market among the young aristocratic Englishmen who spent years, not months, travelling through Italy as part of the Grand Tour. Everywhere they went, from Florence through Rome and Naples to Venice, artists and craftsmen jostled for position among young *milordi* as keen to spend as to learn – and Canaletto was among them from the first.

While building collections of snuff boxes and tapestries, and sitting for portraits by Pompeo Batoni, this influx of young monied patrons led to the creation of an entirely new genre of landscape paintings. Canaletto was one of the leading practitioners and for much of the 1720s and 1730s he had an English promoter as well as English clients. The Venice-based connoisseur and collector Joseph Smith recognized that much of Canaletto's appeal to this particular audience relied on the impressive scale of his works as well as their apparent detail and accuracy, and he marketed his talents accordingly.

Both subject matter and execution tended towards the formulaic, but Canaletto's larger paintings were well suited to the walls of England's newly fashionable neo-Palladian country houses. His fine attention to detail also meant such pictures offered buyers an attractive record of their travels, and did so at a fraction of the cost of a genuine Renaissance master such as Titian, Michelangelo or Raphael.

Even now one wonders was there ever a finer souvenir than a Canaletto, but unfortunately this mutually rewarding Anglo-Italian business relationship was to founder all too soon with the advent of the War of the Austrian Succession (1740–48). As long as the fighting continued, Englishmen were understandably reluctant to risk a tour on the Continent, and so the painter sensibly decided to cut his losses and follow his customers across the Channel to England.

To his critics the move was not necessarily to be rated a success, and the quality of some of Canaletto's English views was considered so poor that for a while he was obliged to work before an audience in order to demonstrate that the painted panels were his and not the daubs of an imposter. However, to the less well-trained eye they are delightful, and Canaletto's views of Eton College, Alnwick and Warwick castles and Surrey's Old Walton Bridge have become as appealing and as popular as much of his Venetian work.

In all he remained in London for nearly a decade, renting a house at 16 Silver Street (now 41 Beak Street) as both his residence and a studio–saleroom. As someone who had built his reputation on urban scenes he quickly turned to his adopted home for inspiration, and completing nearly fifty paintings in all he worked hard to sell them at exhibitions held at his Soho home.

Regardless of the critics' carping, works such as *The Old Horse Guards, St Paul's Cathedral, The Thames from Somerset House Terrace towards the City* and its companion looking towards Westminster give the modern-day viewer

THE PERFECT CHEAT

As an artist Canaletto was entirely happy to move a building, to enlarge or diminish it or to rotate it slightly in order to improve his compositions — no surprise there perhaps: he had trained under his father as a set painter for the theatre. For much the same reason he also arranged for the great unwashed hordes largely to disappear, but we can forgive him this too. Not just because to do otherwise in a city as huge and vital as eighteenth-century London would be to reduce every picture to a crowd scene, but because the human figures he permitted to remain — including one apparently taking a pee in a yard off Whitehall — bring the pictures alive and make them endlessly fascinating for anyone with the time to peruse them properly.

an evocative and colourful view of London in the mid-eighteenth century. Others, notably *Northumberland House* and *Westminster Bridge*, detail some of its more regrettable losses, while a couple of rare interiors bring alive two of the city's most celebrated buildings. The first, of the rococo rotunda at Chelsea's Ranelagh Gardens,* depicts the extraordinarily ornate pleasure dome that played host to a young Mozart, while the second captures Henry VII's chapel at Westminster Abbey in all its soaring Gothic glory.

---

* The owner of the gardens was also Italian, a Jewish immigrant called Solomon Rieti whose great-great nephew was Benjamin Disraeli.

Admittedly much of what we see in his paintings today is not what an eighteenth-century Londoner would have recognized as his home. The grit, social depth and seedy immediacy of his contemporary, Hogarth (see Chapter 45), held no appeal for Canaletto – professionally, at least – and he made no attempt to achieve anything similar. Instead the viewer is treated to a utopian vision of rain-free skies, a pristine river Thames and a complete absence of smog from a million forges and fires. Everything is bathed in a special light, one that – if not quite a Venetian light – gives these images an unmistakable air of unreality but one that nevertheless draws in the viewer.

Canaletto's London, then, may not be the real London, and like many an artist he is an unreliable witness. But his is a London that is somehow familiar, and somewhere most of us – given a Grand Tour and a time machine – would find irresistible to visit.

18. Karl Marx (1818-83)

28 Dean Street, W1

Living in Silver Street Canaletto would have found himself among many of his own countrymen, Soho being an area long characterized by successive waves of immigrants

69

and refugees. French Protestants were among the first to arrive in any number, as many as fifty thousand fleeing persecution after Louis XIV's 1685 revocation of the Edict of Nantes. Greek Street and the area now known as Chinatown can probably speak for themselves, and following the political upheavals of 1848 many hundreds of radicals and would-be revolutionaries poured into this same area from central and eastern Europe.

Among the latter was one Karl Heinrich Marx, a Prussian-born philosopher, economist and revolutionary socialist who arrived in London in 1849. He had already had his work censored by the authorities in Cologne, been expelled from Paris and told he could settle in Brussels only on condition that he refrained from all political writing. The British authorities likewise refused him citizenship but nevertheless let him stay. Presumably hoping London would allow him more intellectual and political freedom (and supported financially by his friend Friedrich Engels) he immediately set about establishing a new base in the city for his Communist League.

By the time of his death Marx was living in modest comfort on the borders of Chalk Farm and Kentish Town, but his most fruitful years in London were these early ones.* It was in Soho that he and wife Jenny rented their

---

* When an official Blue Plaque was installed on the façade of the family home at 41 Maitland Park Road it was damaged by stone-throwing fascist agitators and had to be removed.

MARX: AS INFLUENTIAL AS HE WAS UNLIKEABLE

Intelligent and powerfully driven, Marx himself was otherwise an unattractive character. Thickset and with exceptionally hairy hands, his distinctive broad forehead bore a scar above one eye from a duel during his time at Bonn University in the 1830s. He was also cold, frequently sarcastic, arrogant and conceited, some of the personal attributes that might explain why fewer than a dozen people turned up at his funeral in 1883. (Also why for the next seventy-odd years no one bothered tending his now famous grave at Highgate Cemetery.) Brandy was a favourite when he could find someone else to pay for it – not for him the small beer of the common man – and as erstwhile Labour leader Michael Foot once famously remarked, 'he wasn't a Marxist all the time. He got drunk in the Tottenham Court Road.'

first flat, which was small but convenient for the German Workers' Educational Society that held its meetings in Great Windmill Street. It was also in Soho that he began writing the first volume of *Das Kapital,* the book that was to make his name and – if only temporarily – help change the face of the world.

Their first flat was at 64 Dean Street, a thoroughfare described by a visitor at the time as being one of the worst corners in the whole of London. A short move

a few months later to No. 28 brought no real improve-
ment, even though Marx had secured a paid position in
the meantime as a European correspondent of the *New
York Daily Tribune*. In fact the second flat, above what is
now the restaurant Quo Vadis, was still only two rooms –
'the evil frightful rooms', in the words of Jenny, 'which
encompassed all our joy and all our pain'.

Notwithstanding the meanness and cramped squalor
of his quarters – the couple went on to have seven children, four of them called Jenny – Marx felt able to employ
a maid. (This was Helene Demuth, who subsequently bore
him an eighth child to add to the tally.) Largely absent as
a father he put in long hours, much of it in the circular
reading room at the British Museum. Unfortunately his
earnings from his writing never rose above the meagre,
in large part because he spent far too much time revis-
ing and re-revising texts that failed to see the light of day
until long after his death.

When at last the family could afford to relocate to
somewhere less squalid, it was only as a result of an
inheritance of Jenny's, from her bourgeois father Baron
von Westphalen, and the continuing largesse of Engels.
Sadly, of the seven legitimate Marx offspring only three
lived long enough to make the move, and perhaps even
more tragically two of the three later killed themselves.

Besides being poor for much of his time in London
Marx also became increasingly isolated. Being housebound

because he had pawned his clothes didn't help matters, but he never learned to speak English properly or felt that he belonged here. Neither was he ever to find much solace in journalism, his more than five hundred articles for the *Tribune* being described by their author as 'this continual newspaper muck annoys me. It takes a lot of time, disperses my efforts and in the final analysis is nothing.'

Perhaps even more seriously Marx was never able to accept that the era of revolution had reached its peak in 1848 and was afterwards in decline. Always vigilant for signs that capitalism was finally about to collapse – something he maintained was an absolute inevitability[*] – Marx was equally certain that the overthrow would begin in Britain. That Britain had experienced nothing in 1848 to match the turmoil seen across Europe did nothing to dampen this conviction, and frankly now one wonders what he saw when he looked out of his window and onto the street.

That said, so many years after the fall of the Berlin Wall, and its aftershocks, it is perhaps too easy (and even a little unfair?) to ask whether or not Marx got it wrong. The stark reality is that he did, and not just because he assumed the conditions that produced 1848 could not and would not change without a revolution.

---

[*] 'What the bourgeoisie produces above all, is its own gravediggers.'
– K. Marx

Around him change was happening all the time: the very year *Das Kapital* was published Britain extended the vote to working-class men. But, stubborn to the end, Marx neither foresaw the course of political reform nor acknowledged significant changes when these were made. Capitalists, he continued to insist, were rapacious and destructive and would remain so. The modern appetite for consumerism would have baffled him entirely, while his isolation left him unable to understand England or the English or why almost none of us embraced his ideas.

Elsewhere socialist revolutions did take place, but none were played out according to Marx's model. As we can now see, most met with little or only temporary success, and almost without exception they occurred in politically backward, non-industrialized nations rather than the advanced capitalist economies that Marx so despised.

19. Kate Meyrick (1875-1933)

43 Gerrard Street, W1

A case these days can be made for Peter Stringfellow as the most famous nightclub proprietor in London, but for decades it was Kate Meyrick of the '43'.

Yet Mrs Meyrick cannot with any certainty be called the first. Evelyn Waugh's novelist brother, Alec, is sometimes said to have introduced the cocktail party to London, in April 1924, but the origins of the capital's first nightclub are anyone's guess. With its raffish but wealthy clientele the '43' must have been among them, however, and together with its owner it was by far the most notorious of the roaring twenties.

Almost from the start Kate Meyrick's patrons were mostly society figures, although when her name first made an appearance in the press it was in the crime reports rather than the gossip columns. This was on 28 January 1920, when the Brighton doctor's wife was fined £25 by a magistrate who had described the club where she was arrested as a 'sink of iniquity', before revoking its licence.

The club in question was in Leicester Square, and the outwardly respectable Mrs Meyrick insisted she was working there only to help meet her daughters' school fees. The fine was nevertheless considerable, the equivalent to six weeks' pay for the average working man. The returns from running a Soho nightclub were clearly much greater though, because only a few months later Meyrick was back in business and running a club of her own at 43 Gerrard Street.

Dingy, damp, smoke-filled and ill-lit, the basement of the poet John Dryden's old home was more seedy than glamorous, but for its fashionable clientele this proved more of an attraction than a repellent. So too it seemed did some of Mrs Meyrick's 'edgy' associates, in particular a handsome but reputedly dangerous figure called Brilliant Chang, who was said to be the mastermind behind the extensive Chinese-controlled drug trade in that part of London.

Within weeks of opening, the new club could boast royalty among its members – admittedly only the likes of the King of Egypt's brother to begin with, although younger members of the British royal family were not far behind. By 1924 when Mrs Meyrick was back at Bow Street Court – this time charged with selling intoxicating liquor without a licence – it was noted that her regulars included HRH the Prince of Wales, the future Edward VIII. On that occasion she was fined forty shillings and jailed for six months, and was joined in the dock by more than thirty men and eight other women who had been apprehended in the same raid.

These were relatively minor crimes and the sentences far from exceptional, but her notoriety was assured the following year when the Home Secretary fainted during a reception at Buckingham Palace. The cause of his collapse was put down to stress due to overwork, after which the Rt Hon Sir William Joynson-Hicks confirmed that the long hours had been spent largely in a determined effort to destroy Mrs Meyrick.

The publicity for the '43' must have been invaluable, as indeed was the news a few months later that her daughter Dorothy had run off with Edward Southwell Russell, 26th Baron de Clifford. Marriage into the aristocracy caused excitement enough, but then Lord de Clifford was himself charged with an offence when it was revealed that the secret marriage had taken place without parental consent. As he was still only nineteen, de Clifford was fined £50 by the Lord Mayor of London.*

Mrs Meyrick made no public comment on the affair, and in due course a second daughter married the Earl of Craven and a third the Earl of Kinnoull. Buoyed up by such smart associations business was booming, and when a new club called the Silver Slipper was raided by police on Christmas Day 1927 it surprised no one that she was the owner. Located in more upmarket Regent Street this latest club had a stylish glass dance floor, and besides this venue Mrs Meyrick also confessed to an interest in the Manhattan in nearby Denman Street and the Folies-Bergères in Newman Street.

Once more, several members of her staff were arrested on various minor charges, and the following June Mrs Meyrick was herself in trouble after pleading guilty to

_____

* Lord de Clifford was famously back in court in 1935. Following a fatal road accident in Surrey he became the last peer ever to be tried in the House of Lords. Interestingly he had succeeded to the title as a consequence of another traffic accident that had claimed the life of his father a quarter of a century earlier.

selling alcohol again at the '43' and without a licence. Though tearful and apparently contrite, she was nevertheless portrayed by the prosecuting barrister as 'the most inveterate lawbreaker with regard to licensing matters that the [London] police have ever dealt with' – and sentenced to another six months behind bars.

Released from Holloway in November, she made a big splash after being met at the gates by the new Countess of Kinnoull, and hosted a lavish welcome-home party for herself at the Silver Slipper. Alas, less than two weeks later, Kate Meyrick was named on a new arrest warrant, this time for the far more serious charge of perverting the course of justice by bribing a police officer.

Physically her decline can be dated from this point, and before long one of her offspring was petitioning the Home Secretary to secure her early release. Nothing came of this, and she served her sentence before returning for a fourth and then a fifth stay as guest of His Majesty. On both occasions she was found guilty of contravening the liquor laws, after which there was some talk of a new venture in Monte Carlo, perhaps because life in London was becoming too hot for her to handle.

Finally in May 1929 came news that the '43' might close for good, its licence permanently revoked, and that the queen of London's nightclub scene was abdicating. 'She is in far from good health', said a friend, and the strain was beginning to show.

THE PROTOTYPE FOR
METROPOLITAN POLICE
CORRUPTION

The most incriminating piece of evidence against Meyrick came in 1927, a safety deposit box in the name of Vice Squad Detective Sergeant George Goddard. Conceivably the first in the long run of bent coppers operating in Soho, Goddard had led the first raid on the '43' several years earlier, since when he had somehow amassed a personal fortune of £12,000. Most of it was in bundles of £10 notes stored in the box, and in court it transpired that at a time when a chief constable could expect to be paid £800–£1,000 per year, Goddard had been collecting five times this amount, up to £100 per week, in protection money. Despite her protestations that she had no knowledge of any of this, much of Goddard's retirement fund had clearly come from Mrs Meyrick. She was soon back in Holloway, this time for fifteen months of hard labour.

Kate Meyrick retired to the country to work on her memoirs, and then, still a couple of years shy of sixty, she died suddenly of bronchopneumonia and was buried quietly after a funeral at St Martin-in-the-Fields. Her book was promptly banned and has never seen the light of day. The certainty is that nothing in it would have shocked a London clubber today, but there was a time when names needed protecting and, if nothing else, Mrs Meyrick had known them all.

20. John Logie Baird (1888-1946)

22 Frith Street, W1

Who now remembers the name of William Taynton? In late 1924 an obscure Scottish inventor rented a couple of attic rooms in Soho after being evicted from his south coast lodgings by a landlord worried that he was going to burn down the building. A year or so later, in January 1926, he successfully transmitted a moving image of an unknown office boy, twenty-year-old William Taynton. Fast forward a quarter of a century and the latter – the first man on TV, but still not famous – was back in Frith Street to unveil a plaque commemorating the invention of what Baird called the televisor, and what a sceptical press described as 'seeing by wireless'.

It seems incredible now but, having pioneered one of only very few machines that can genuinely be said to have changed the world, John Logie Baird had an incredibly hard time convincing the world of its value.

Calling on Lord Beaverbrook's popular *Daily Express* he had been dismissed as a madman and quickly shown the door. *The Times* at least accepted his assertion that it was possible to reproduce moving pictures in this way, but its reporter was quick to express his disappointment at the quality of the images, which he found blurred and indistinct.

Baird's track record as an inventor was unimpressive, however, and wouldn't have inspired much confidence. He had come up with a simple telephone exchange he claimed to have rigged up in his bedroom as a teenager. This enabled him to speak to chums across the street, but more recent money-making schemes had all ended in failure. Also, a new type of razor blade he'd invented was indeed rustproof, but being made of glass it broke and cut the user's face, while an idea for pneumatic shoes based on semi-inflated balloons led the wearer in what Baird himself described as 'a succession of drunken and uncontrollable lurches' before one of them burst.

Initially it looked like this new televisor might go the same way, displaying as it did the unmistakable quality of something cobbled together at home using anything that came to hand. Identifiable components included an old hatbox, scissors, darning needles, lenses from several bicycle lamps, sealing wax and an old tea chest – but then transmission of moving pictures was a dream that so many boffins had been working on for so many

81

RETAIL RIDES TO THE RESCUE

Happily the eponymous owner of one of London's most fashionable stores could see some value in Baird's experimentations, and Harry Gordon Selfridge (see Chapter 2) confirmed his intention to display the televisor in his store if the inventor could build more of them. Alive to the potential for publicity he insisted the machine's creator should be on hand on the sales floor personally to demonstrate the device to any potential buyers, and Baird moved into position for the next three weeks.

years, which presumably explains why a reported fifty scientists (all of them members and fellows of the Royal Institution) were soon queueing to witness Baird's first public demonstration.

Baird was also developing this new technology with incredible rapidity. Initially he could broadcast flickering images for only a few feet, but he had soon stretched the working range to well over four hundred miles – equivalent, in other words, to the distance between the attic in Soho and his home town of Helensburgh. Before very long he was able to beam pictures across the Atlantic *in colour*, and later still to transmit images that were stereoscopic.

By 1928 his new Baird Television Development Company had made its first television programme for the new BBC (broadcasting from the high ground at Alexandra Palace). In 1929 Baird helped to establish Télévision-Baird-Natan, the first television network in France, with Germany joining the party around the same time after the Post Office there provided the facilities Baird needed to develop its first television service.

Along with the 1931 Epsom Derby (the first-ever outdoor sports broadcast) these were significant landmarks and in retrospect it seems entirely fitting that what remains the definitive medium for public entertainment should have had its origins in Soho, an area very much associated with having fun. The reality, however, is that as with so many things in London – the Tube most obviously, and a crumbling labyrinth of Victorian sewers – first rarely means the best and Baird's invention was no exception.

Adopting a mechanical system had enabled the Scotsman to beat his rivals to first base, but his technology was very quickly superseded by much more advanced alternatives. In particular, a generation of new electronic systems was being developed by Marconi in America, and while Baird was experimenting with something similar he was heavily outfinanced and then outpaced by the larger company. When a BBC committee of inquiry conducted trials between the British product and its US rival in the mid-1930s Baird's system was found wanting, and was very quickly dropped.

Baird was down but not quite out, and in the following years was associated with advances made in video recording, colour imagery, fibre optics and even an early form of 3D TV. There is also a suggestion that he played a key role in the development of radar, but this has been disputed and, with much of its history cloaked in wartime secrecy, has never been verified.

Chapter 5

COVENT GARDEN AND STRAND

21. Pietro Gimonde, aka Signor Bologna (c.1600s)

Covent Garden Piazza, WC2

Pietro Gimonde – or Signor Bologna as he was most commonly known to London audiences – brought the comedy of Italy to the heart of the capital. Through a version of the traditional *commedia dell'arte*, and his invocation of the devious Polichinella, Gimonde brought a show to London in 1662 that Samuel Pepys found 'very pretty, the best that ever I saw, and a great resort of gallants'. The diarist's small review unknowingly went on to mark the birth of the British tradition that we know as Punch and Judy.

The character of Punch was derived from the stock character of Polichinella, a Neapolitan whose crafty, vicious ways were depicted as fundamental to his working-class situation. Polichinella was a man who, having nothing left to lose, resorted to violence and cunning to find his amusement. Stripped of his wealth, happiness and status, Polichinella appealed to the London masses through his rambunctious resolve to get whatever he wanted by any means necessary – cue the numerous blows to any opponents from his now-famous cudgel.

However, in an attempt to appeal more to a British audience, Gimonde's London show underwent some modifications. The simplest and most enduring of these was the name switch from Polichinella to Punchinanello, then again to Punchinello and eventually, and in a phrase easy enough for Londoners to get their tongues around, simply Mr Punch. Such changes were also evident in Punch's wife, as the classic Joan was in time swapped for a simpler and perhaps more modern Judy.

The success of Gimonde was not solely reserved for the thronging crowds of commoners at Covent Garden market; the king himself was also said to have enjoyed his talents. Calling upon Gimonde to perform his famous sketch, not once but three times according to some reports, Charles II eventually gave Gimonde a gold chain and medal worth £25 (£3,000 today) for his excellent showmanship. As many others later would do, Gimonde proved that despite being a foreigner, and presenting a show that cruelly mocked the lower order of society, he had what it took to perform for the king.

For the numerous jesters, street entertainers and performers that followed in the footsteps of Gimonde, the unchanging phrase 'That's the way to do it', traditionally said every time Punch administers a blow with his baton to an unsuspecting victim, remains part of the legacy left by Gimonde.

22. Samuel Johnson (1709-84)

8 Russell Street, WC2

The plaque mounted high on the façade of No. 8 Russell Street is unusual in that it commemorates a meeting rather than the home or workplace of an eminent person. It is not unique in London, however, as there is another on the exterior wall of Bart's Hospital museum. Where that one marks the coming together of two fictional characters – Sherlock Holmes and Dr Watson – the Covent Garden plaque celebrates actual people, both highly significant figures in the literary life of eighteenth-century London, who met in 1763.

The two in question are the great lexicographer Samuel Johnson and his biographer James Boswell, neither of whom was a Londoner. James Boswell hailed from Edinburgh and in due course succeeded his father as the 9th Laird of Auchinleck. Johnson was from the English Midlands, the son of a Lichfield bookseller, who left Oxford without a degree and worked as a tutor before travelling to London in 1737 with a former pupil called David Garrick.

Garrick had already shown promise as an actor and had good social connections in London, but Johnson had none and his prospects were not as good. He had not been a success as a teacher, many of his younger pupils becoming alarmed by his habit of 'distorting his face' and gesticulating wildly (probably a symptom of Tourette's syndrome). With no trade or profession on which to capitalize he was soon penniless, and seemed unemployable before managing to secure a post as a writer for *The Gentleman's Magazine*.

At the time this was published from the old gatehouse of the Priory of the Knights of St John in Clerkenwell, and as a hack Johnson's work was hugely varied. His intelligence never in doubt, he was both industrious and fast, his output including plays and poetry as well as a biography of his late friend and fellow poet Richard Savage.

Confident of his abilities, after being contracted to produce his famous dictionary in 1746 Johnson agreed to complete the task for fifteen hundred guineas and to publish within three years. In the event it took him nine, but so immense was the task (nearly forty-three thousand definitions supported by many thousands of quotations) that even this was taken as proof of his talents and Johnson himself liked to joke that the French equivalent had taken forty scholars from the Académie française more than forty years.

First or not, the dictionary made an immediate hero of its creator, and described by Tobias Smollett as 'the Great Cham [or khan] of Literature' Johnson was quickly awarded a Crown pension of £300 per year by way of thanks. Inevitably not everyone shared Smollett's view, however, and far from seeing Johnson as the foremost

THE BEST BUT NOT THE FIRST

Contrary to popular belief, the dictionary for which Johnson is so famous was neither the first in the English language nor the most extensive: around twenty such publications had appeared in the preceding hundred years, at least one of which defined a greater number of words than Johnson managed to do. Johnson's was the best, however, and by far the most widely used, despite a price equivalent today to around £350. As such it quickly set an entirely new standard and one that – incredibly – remained in place until well into the twentieth century when the first *Oxford English Dictionary* appeared.

figure in literary London, Macaulay later considered him to be just a 'wretched etymologist'.

Its success meant that Johnson was no longer poor, but he continued to cut a fairly grotesque figure. Physically shambolic and, as Boswell later observed, having 'no passion for clean linen', he still displayed numerous strange tics and mannerisms such as counting his footsteps (even when riding on horseback), muttering to himself and exhaling loudly at the end of his long, meandering speeches.

Always a big eater and with table manners that one contemporary likened to those of a cormorant, Johnson's appetite for prodigious quantities of 'bishop' (a mixture of port, sugar and orange) eventually gave way to a liking for tea, of which he would drink more than two dozen cups at one sitting. He was also something of a hypochondriac, and took opium daily for many years to help with various ailments both real and imagined.

By the time the meeting with Boswell took place, appropriately enough over more tea in the premises of a Strand bookseller, Johnson was well into middle age and had been a widower for ten years. Boswell was already keeping a journal of his time in London, although this wasn't generally known until the mid-twentieth century. In it, the twenty-two-year-old describes the meeting and his efforts to conceal his Scottishness because he recognized Johnson's 'most dreadful appearance' and knew of his 'mortal antipathy' to anyone from north of the border.

Finding Johnson 'very slovenly in his dress and [speaking] with a most uncouth voice' Boswell nevertheless appreciated the older man's knowledge, humour and worth. His decision to record the great man's words and deeds, and indeed his thoughts, grew out of this respect for him and his work, and in retrospect can be said to have laid the foundations for the modern biography.

It was Johnson who advised Boswell that it was 'by studying little things that we attain the great knowledge of having as little misery and as much happiness as possible' – and by studying these little things in turn that Boswell realized, perhaps unconsciously, that one *builds up* a picture of a great person such as Johnson. In place of hagiography, Boswell used this realization to present a full and rounded picture of an individual, drawing on his own journal entries and experiences as well as the testimonies of others to produce a fascinating account of Johnson's life and person.

There is some polishing that goes on so that, for example, the description of Johnson in the book is less harsh than the one given in Boswell's private journal. But his *Life of Samuel Johnson* is what it says it is – a life – and is conceivably the first in history to deal with its subject warts and all (or, in Johnson's case perhaps, the facial scars from his childhood scrofula).

Indeed, so determined was Boswell to ensure that the reader was 'well acquainted' with Dr Johnson that he went to great lengths to record not just what was said but *how* it was said. Thus, at times Johnson is described as looking dismal as he talks, or exclaiming something loudly and with passion. Today perhaps we take such things for granted, but 250 years ago Boswell's approach was genuinely revolutionary. Bringing its subject truly to life, Boswell's *Life* enables the reader not merely to become 'well acquainted' with Johnson but also with the London that Johnson knew and with those who clustered around him in the clubs and taverns of Fleet Street in the 1760s.

23. Madame Fahmy (1890-1971)

Savoy Hotel, Strand, WC2

A bloody murder at a famous London hotel is always going to be newsworthy. Throw in a title, more than a hint of sexual perversion, and the kind of scenario likely to appeal to the inherent prejudices of the average Londoner in the 1920s and the resulting cocktail will prove irresistible to newspaper editors and readers alike.

This was certainly the case in July 1923 when French-born Marguerite Fahmy was charged with the murder of a fabulously rich Egyptian princeling called Ali Kamel Fahmy Bey. When he was found shot to death there was little doubt that his wife was responsible: she had the gun; it was covered in her prints; she had even confessed to shooting her husband before being escorted round the corner to Bow Street Magistrates' Court. What makes this particular case so remarkable is that despite the overwhelming evidence against her, the former Parisian prostitute was acquitted and walked free.

Ahead of this the press loved every minute of it, and pored over the tiniest details of the case as they emerged. For example, the deceased was said to be worth more than £2 million – a sum that one could multiply by at least forty today – and newspaper reports of Fahmy's first court appearance made much of Madame's expensive Chanel dress and her diamond and emerald jewellery. The couple had been married for well under a year, and it was clear that the thirty-three-year-old Frenchwoman was an accomplished gold-digger and that her relationship with the handsome twenty-two-year-old Egyptian had been fiery from the very start.

Amidst much talk of fights both in private and in public, Fahmy had reportedly summoned a doctor to the couple's suite soon after their arrival in London in order to examine injuries that she insisted were the result of her husband's attempts to engage her in 'unnatural' intercourse. Also, following the shooting, various unnamed hotel guests were happy to confirm that the victim had been seen around the Savoy's bars and restaurants with cuts to his face that were suggestive of a cat fight.

On 9 July the couple had gone to the theatre together, as it happens to see *The Merry Widow*. On returning to the hotel witnesses saw them arguing loudly in the hotel's famous grill room, the maître d' eventually having to calm both down for fear that one or other would reach for the empty wine bottle on the table to use it as a weapon. Madame Fahmy apparently left the table first, and went up alone to their suite.

Guests were woken a few hours later by the sound

of three shots coming from the couple's bedroom. On investigating the source of the commotion the night porter found the Egyptian bleeding profusely from his head, his wife leaning over him, the gun on the floor, saying repeatedly '*Qu'est-ce que j'ai fait, mon cher?*' ('What have I done, my dear?').

Bailed to appear the following September, one might have imagined her fate to be sealed. She had a motive, she had an illegal lethal weapon in her possession, and at no point had she made any attempt to deny that she had discharged this at close quarters in the direction of her late husband. But to assume the murder of Ali Kamel Fahmy Bey was an open-and-shut case would be grossly to underestimate the natural imbalance of the British legal system, and the talents – if indeed that is the term – of one of its leading advocates, Sir Edward Marshall Hall, KC.

In a system that seems still to favour the person who arrives in court with the largest armoury, Fahmy's choice of one of the country's most expensive lawyers was of course the key to her eventual acquittal. As for Sir Edward, his chief skill in this case – and not for the first time or the last – was to acknowledge that an English jury was likely to be profoundly racist and he was to trade on this at every possible turn. His behaviour in court has been described as a bravura performance, albeit only by his fellow lawyers. To the rest of us it might be seen as obnoxious in the extreme, and grossly dishonest.

Hall dismissed the murder victim as violent, sinister and disgusting, a foreigner with 'abnormal tendencies' that he had forced upon a poor, defenceless and innocent white woman who had suffered 'the tortures of the damned'. An oriental given to a life of debauchery and his own sexual prowess – hints were made about an illegal relationship with his male secretary – the dead man was to be considered beneath contempt. Far from tragic, his premature and violent death was depicted as a blessing for all right-thinking Londoners.

Disgracefully the judge was no better, allowing on the one hand a description to stand of the deceased's household as 'numerous ugly, black, half-civilized man-servants' conspiring against every Christian virtue, while on the other refusing permission for the prosecution even to cross-examine Madame Fahmy. Advising the jury that 'we in this country put our women on a pedestal [but] in Egypt they have not the same views', it is easy to imagine the judge nodding complacently as Sir Edward implored the all-white jury 'to open the gate and let this white woman go back into the light of God's great Western sun'.

The jury, needless to say, was quick to comply with this request and, to the fury of the Egyptian ambassador to the Court of St James's, Fahmy walked: a free woman, in spite of everything. In the tinderbox that was the Middle East following the dismantling of Ottoman rule, educated opinion was outraged at such high-handed behaviour within the British legal system and appalled at both the verdict and the details of a case in which descriptions of Egyptians' supposed backwardness, barbarism and lack of principle had not merely gone unquestioned but been considered wholly acceptable.

Incredibly, Fahmy made a bid to secure her husband's inheritance after her acquittal, but this was quickly rebuffed and she returned to Paris with her reputation in ruins. The picture that remains of her is ugly in the extreme: a woman who had slept her way out of the gutter, exchanging sexual favours with scores of different men in order to claw her way through the various layers of London society before finally ensnaring her prince. Ordinarily such a curriculum vitae would have seen any jury turn on her, but her good fortune was to be white – and to the judiciary's lasting shame that was all Sir Edward needed to know.

24. Ivor Novello (1893-1951)

Former Strand Theatre, 11 Aldwych, WC2

It is a rare jailbird who has a London theatre named in his honour, but decades after his premature death the composer and actor we know as Ivor Novello still casts a uniquely long shadow over the West End.

The prison sentence was a relatively short one but in 1944 it came as a shock to many when Cardiff-born David Ivor Davies was sent down for eight weeks. He served four in Wormwood Scrubs; his offence was one against wartime rationing regulations in that the accused had kept his Rolls-Royce running using petrol coupons supplied to him by a besotted fan who had stolen them from her own employer.

Together with Noël Coward, Novello was at this time one of the real darlings of the theatre world, but his mental health suffered badly as a result of his incarceration and his reputation never quite recovered. Certainly Coward made no attempt to defend his actions, accusing Novello of 'fighting like a steer to keep going as before the war' and doing little if anything for the war effort. Novello's return to the stage after his release won him a standing ovation, but his best years were behind him, and his mass appeal was never quite the same. In all likelihood the incident also cost him a knighthood.

He should be remembered, even so, as one of the twentieth century's leading composers of British musicals, indeed as the dominant force until the appearance many years later of Andrew (now Lord) Lloyd-Webber. Like Lloyd-Webber he came from a musical family, and his mother was an internationally renowned singing teacher who moved the family to London. Taking lodgings at 55 New Bond Street, she was able to introduce her son to performers such as Clara Butt and to theatre manager George Edwardes, who is widely credited with heralding a new era in musical theatre.

Even without such useful connections, however, Novello had a natural talent from an early age. He published his first song before his sixteenth birthday and after leaving school worked briefly in Wales as a singing teacher like his mother. In 1913 he returned to London, by which time the twenty-year-old's royalties enabled him to take on a flat above what was then the Strand Theatre in Aldwych. It was to be his London address for the rest of his life.

The following year Novello penned the music to 'Keep the Home Fires Burning', a song whose sentiment so perfectly captured the mood at the start of the Great War, of soldiers and their sweethearts, that the composer was rapidly catapulted into the limelight. The song is estimated to have earned him around £15,000 (equivalent to well over a million today), but Novello's own war was to be noticeably less glorious: crashing twice whilst training to become a pilot, in 1916 he was manoeuvred into a safer desk job at the Air Ministry by influential friends.

His first stage success also came in 1916, a joint effort between Novello, Jerome Kern and George Grossmith Jr, son and nephew of the bestselling authors of the novel *The Diary of a Nobody* (1892). It was around this time too that the composer met actor Bobbie Andrews, the two of them becoming lovers and remaining together until Novello's death some thirty-five years later.

It was Andrews who was to introduce Novello to Coward outside a hotel in Manchester. Their first meeting was not a success, but Coward later admitted how much he had been awed by 'the magic atmosphere' of Novello's world and the way in which he 'moved and breathed with such nonchalance'.

Hearing this it is hard not to conclude that to some degree Coward, who was six years younger, must have modelled himself on his new friend. Of course, Coward was an actor who turned to writing, whereas for Novello the transition was the other way round, moving from the theatre to star in silent movies as well as talkies. But both successfully made their mark as performers on stage and screen as well as off it, and each was blessed with the kind of voice and profile that fans on both sides of the Atlantic looked for in their favourite matinée idols.

Naturally the two were rivals as well as friends, although they came to blows only once – when Coward punched the Welshman after finding him in tears following Neville Chamberlain's return from Berlin bearing Hitler's worthless piece of paper. As this suggests it was an uneasy relationship, following Novello's early and sudden death (from a heart attack) Coward admitted to his diary that writing a tribute to the deceased for one of the newspapers was 'rather sad and difficult to do'.

Coward may not have appreciated the degree to which his own fame would eclipse that of the older man, but this has certainly been the case. Novello has his theatre, his name lives on in Britain's most prestigious songwriting awards, and an astonishing seven thousand people turned out for his funeral. But London has a Noël Coward Theatre too (the Albery was renamed in 2006), and his plays are subject to endless revival – unlike the rather stagey and dated productions of his former rival.

Today, as a result, Novello the man has been somewhat lost, and like Rudolph Valentino (with whom he was frequently and favourably compared) he is recalled if at all more for the way in which his name evokes a certain lost glamour than for anything he actually achieved. Without doubt he deserves a better fate, but then *sic transit gloria...*

Chapter 6

HOLBORN AND BLOOMSBURY

25. Sir Hans Sloane (1660-1753)

4 Bloomsbury Place, WC1

His name commemorated in numerous streets and squares in north Chelsea (an area that two hundred years ago was even called Hans Town), the physician, scientist and collector-connoisseur arguably made an even bigger mark in Bloomsbury, where he was to become the principal benefactor of the new British Museum.

A popular and successful medical practitioner (in part perhaps because he was a pioneering advocate of the benefits of milk chocolate), Sloane was Irish born and educated in France and the Netherlands. He settled in

Bloomsbury in his mid-thirties and remained in the same house until his retirement nearly fifty years later, although his rapidly growing collections required the addition of the house next door in which to display them. Thereafter his retirement was spent in Chelsea, then situated well outside London, where as Lord of the Manor he owned the old Duke of Beaufort's house and another built for Henry VIII.

Servants at both were dismissive of the ninety-two-year-old's 'collections of gimcracks' but these comprised vast numbers of rare specimens – flora and fauna – which together with hoards of ancient manuscripts, *incunabula* and more than thirty thousand books were to form the founding bequest of the British Museum when this was established in the year of Sloane's death. (Two significant offshoots, the British Library and the Natural History Museum, were also to benefit, although at the time there were not yet plans to establish either.)

Sloane's gift to the nation came with strings, however, a price of £20,000 being mentioned in his will in order to benefit the only two of his children who had survived infancy. At a time when the head of the army was paid £10 per day, and when Sloane's favourite drinking chocolate cost just five shillings per pound, this was a truly astonishing sum. It has since been suggested that the true value of the collection was much higher, however: closer to £50,000, or equivalent to around £80 million in today's terms.

That an individual had managed to establish such a valuable collection says much about Sloane as both a scientist and physician. As the former he had started young, as a child amassing hundreds of botanical specimens for classification and study, and in later life succeeding Sir Isaac Newton as president of the Royal Society. His medical career was similarly impressive. Building up a large and fashionable practice, Sloane attended to patients including Queen Anne, George I and George II; and as well as taking on another influential presidency (that of the Royal College of Physicians) Sloane's 1716 baronetcy marked the first time that a medical practitioner had been given an hereditary title.

Even allowing for the £20,000 payment, Sloane's bequest in Bloomsbury must still stand as one of the most remarkable and most generous acts of philanthropy in British history and, following the acceptance of the offer made by his will, Parliament passed a special Foundation Act agreeing to purchase the collections from his executors. The same act allowed a further £10,000 to be spent acquiring hundreds more manuscripts from the Duchess of Portland, and called for funds to design and construct 'one general repository for the better reception of the said collections'. Much of the latter was to come from a public lottery, and £10,250 was used to purchase Montague House in Bloomsbury, which opened to the public in 1759.

CHELSEA:
SLOANE'S SECOND LEGACY

Earnings from his medical practice were wisely invested, Sloane acquiring property in Chelsea at a fraction of its eventual value (Beaufort House was more or less a ruin, but enviably situated) and purchasing important scientific specimens from other collectors around Europe. The land was to prove a particularly shrewd purchase, and much of Sloane's 250 acre estate is still in private hands centuries later. The bulk of this descended via one of his daughters who married into the Cadogan family with the result that the 8th Earl Cadogan is today one of London's largest and richest landlords, second only to his neighbour the Duke of Westminster.

Sloane leased a very small portion of the estate and later bequeathed it to the Worshipful Society of Apothecaries, which created a four-acre walled physic garden to assist the training of its apprentices. The second oldest of its type in England (after Oxford) this delightful, hidden enclave is open to the public and its gentle microclimate continues to allow more than five thousand edible, medicinal and historical specimens to flourish.

Initially the new museum was open for just three hours a day, and would-be visitors first had to apply in writing. Even then tickets were issued most grudgingly, at a rate of just ten per hour, and it was to be 120 years before the sort of unrestricted access visitors now take for granted became the norm.

It was obvious, even so, that the new premises were grossly inadequate and soon temporary structures began to spring up in the courtyard behind the old house. These too were soon shown to be insufficient, however, as the Sloane collections were rapidly joined by several others. These included more than 130,000 books from the Royal Library, some fantastic Napoleonic plunder such as the hugely significant Rosetta Stone, and the Royal Society's own Museum of Curiosities. By the 1830s it was clear that new bespoke premises were required, and barely a decade later the duke's old house was torn down to make way for the vast and majestic storehouse that forms the cultural heart of modern-day Bloomsbury.

London without the British Museum is hard to imagine today, although most visitors arrive knowing nothing of Sir Hans Sloane – and many leave much the same. Without his example, however, the place would not exist in the form we have all come to know and love. There were museums before this one: Ashburnham House in Westminster was full of books and antiquities; in Queen Anne's Gate visitors could see Charles Townley's world-class collection of classical sculptures. But it was Sloane's vision that set in train the developments needed to create a truly great national repository and research centre, and his collections formed the nucleus of what remains one of the two or three finest museums anywhere in the world.

26. Hon. Henry Cavendish (1731-1810)

11 Bedford Square, WC1

Whilst perhaps the earliest prototype for the popular idea of a mad scientist, the rich life of Henry Cavendish nevertheless represents an important strand in the history of science, with Cavendish the kind of industrious and profoundly gifted gentleman-amateur on whom much pioneering work depended.

At the time his specialism was called natural philosophy, although today Cavendish would be described as an experimental physicist and chemist. His talents and commitment led to the discovery of hydrogen, or as he knew it 'inflammable air', and nitric acid. He was also able to calculate with considerable accuracy the relative density and therefore total weight of the earth.

With both his grandfathers being dukes his was a privileged upbringing, although his mother died when he was just two years old. Educated in London and at Peterhouse, Cambridge, Cavendish followed his father into the Royal Society and its associated dining club. At the latter his behaviour was from the start eccentric, and while he would rarely miss a dinner he was known never to initiate a conversation with any of his fellow members. Indeed, if spoken to he would only squeak in response, or mumble unintelligibly if he found the topic of conversation particularly interesting.

At home he was even less communicative, and preferred to write letters to his servants rather than addressing them directly. (There is also an account, now impossible to verify, that he had additional staircases constructed in order to avoid bumping into servants unexpectedly.) Not surprisingly he never married, but still maintained two large fully staffed houses within just a few miles of each other, the interiors of each being painted a uniform and unrelenting green.

The one in Bloomsbury Cavendish filled with more than twelve thousand books and journals of science, an important resource that he generously shared with other scientists who were permitted to visit and borrow from it as if it were a public library. (Curiously Cavendish also insisted on filling out the requisite forms whenever he wished to refer to one of his own books.) An even larger villa on Clapham Common he set aside for his scientific enquiries, constructing a series of private laboratories that gradually took over both the house and garden.

Neither place could have been described as homely, and female staff in particular ran the risk of being dismissed if they surprised their employer by suddenly appearing in his view. But the library was of international standing and the laboratories superbly well equipped, thanks to an inheritance that left Cavendish one of the richest commoners in England – or as was once said 'the richest of the learned and the most learned of the rich'.

Notwithstanding the odd personal behaviour he was universally acclaimed by his peers, Sir Humphry Davy's description being typical of many in identifying him as 'acute, sagacious, and profound, and, I think, the most accomplished British philosopher of his time'. Some of his experiments would seem to us now to be a trifle bizarre – to measure an electric current he would shock himself before estimating how much agony he experienced – but his work was in general meticulously well planned and painstakingly executed.

Above all it was Cavendish who pioneered the study of gases, developing practical methods for collecting and weighing them at a time when doing so posed many challenges. Hydrogen, for example, is colourless, tasteless, invisible – and extremely hazardous to work with – and while today even children know that water is a compound of two gases, at the time Cavendish succeeded in isolating one of them it was the first time in history that an element had been identified. That he managed to weigh it is also remarkable, given the relative crudity of his equipment as compared to the sort of kit that is available today.

It is true that, like many at the leading edge of scientific exploration, he made mistakes, and certainly he failed fully to grasp the significance and implications of some of his own discoveries. Unfortunately he was also highly reluctant to publish his research (much of which saw the light of day only after his death) and of course his reclusive personality and pathological shyness made it impossible for him to share and discuss developing ideas with others working in the same field.

As a result, Henry Cavendish remains something of an unsung hero, but in truth he deserves to stand alongside the likes of Newton, Darwin and Einstein as one of the few men in history who change things for ever. For literally thousands of years, since classical times, it had been accepted that our world comprised just four things: earth, air, fire and water. But working alone in green-painted seclusion Cavendish changed all that at a stroke.

Observing that hydrogen reacted with oxygen to form water – each time he put a light to his 'inflammable air' moisture would form on the surface of the glass vessel in which it was held – Cavendish realized that water could not therefore be an element. From this small realization, an authentic eureka moment, sprang an entirely new age of rational, experimental science, an age we live in still.

27. Charles Darwin (1809-82)

110 Gower Street, WC1

The great naturalist spent the early years of his married life living in a small rented house on the site of what is now part of University College London, the institution that has grown to dominate this end of the street for close on two hundred years. In 1838 when he took on the lease the correct address for the furnished property was No. 12 Upper Gower Street, but Darwin always referred to it as 'Macaw Cottage', a reference to the furniture and décor that according to one of his daughters 'combined all the colours of the macaw in hideous discord'.

By Darwin's own account it was the ugliest building, and a dead dog presumably owned by the previous tenant was found lying in the garden when he took on the lease. He was nevertheless delighted to have got it and wrote excitedly to his fiancée (and first cousin) Emma Wedgwood to tell her the good news.* He moved into the house on the last day of 1838, just weeks after their

---

* Both were grandchildren of the celebrated potter Josiah Wedgwood, and having known each other since childhood the pair were married by a third cousin, John Allen Wedgwood.

engagement was made public, and Emma joined him there when they married less than a month later.

Darwin had first arrived in London around two years earlier to make arrangements for the safe storage and display of the collections he had made on the *Beagle* expedition. (Acquired from as far afield as South America, Africa and Australasia, most of the bones and fossils eventually found their way to the now Royal College of Surgeons in Lincoln's Inn Fields.) Whilst living in lodgings in Great Marlborough Street – at that time an address much favoured by doctors and architects – he was also able to secure a grant of £1,000 from public funds towards the publication of several volumes of *The Zoology of the Voyage of H.M.S. Beagle.* Simultaneously he reluctantly accepted the secretaryship of the Geological Society, a post that he occupied until 1841.

Born and raised in the Midlands, and educated at Edinburgh and Cambridge, Darwin took to London immediately, enjoying what he called the 'grandeur about its smoky fogs, and the dull, distant sounds of cabs and coaches' and telling a friend 'you may perceive I am becoming a thorough-going cockney'. Unfortunately his health – which was never good – eventually necessitated a move to the country, a combination of gout and Chagas disease contracted during his *Beagle* days leaving him prone to repeated bouts of debilitating illness. Because of this – and with the Gower Street house torn down after being badly damaged by enemy action in 1940 – it is Down House in Kent that has today become most associated with the great man and his work.

The few short years that Darwin and his wife spent in London were to be highly significant ones, however. *On the Origin of Species by Means of Natural Selection* may not have seen the light of day until 1859, but much of the groundwork for the theories behind it was done while the Darwins lived in Bloomsbury. Especially when revisited in *The Descent of Man* (1871), which applied many of the same ideas to human beings, these theories genuinely electrified Victorian society.

Then, as now, his ideas divided opinion. Those such as the philosopher and historian Thomas Carlyle took the greatest exception to 'these gorilla damnifactions of humanity'. But others welcomed them with open arms, including Karl Marx who wanted to dedicate the English translation of *Das Kapital* to their instigator and would have had not Darwin personally declined the honour. Few books have made such an impact before or since, and for this reason alone the loss of the house in which the ideas took shape is to be regretted. (There is at least some justice in the choice of its replacement, which houses part of UCL's Department of Biological Sciences.)

THE STRONGEST CHALLENGE
TO A LADY'S FAITH

Years before she married Darwin, Emma Wedgwood was already a strong supporter of his ambitions and is known, for example, to have been instrumental in helping to overturn considerable family objections to his plans to join the survey ship HMS *Beagle* on its five-year expedition beginning in 1831. This support continued throughout their marriage, and did so despite her own deeply held religious views.

Raised as a Unitarian her faith was the result of much thought and study, and Darwin felt obliged to confess his own growing religious scepticism when proposing marriage. Emma seemed to welcome this honesty and openness, believing fervently that anyone 'acting conscientiously and sincerely wishing and trying to learn the truth' could not be wholly wrong.

Recognizing that Darwin's work posed a serious challenge to her own beliefs, she hoped that if they were open and honest in their discussions it would bring them closer together rather than forcing them apart. In this she seems to have been proved largely correct in that, while significant differences were never resolved, a bond was certainly forged by their lengthy and honest discussions. (The same, alas, cannot be said for Admiral FitzRoy, the commander of the *Beagle* and an ardent creationist who claimed to have suffered 'the acutest pain' as a consequence of Darwin's explosive theories.)

Besides its connection to *Origins* Macaw Cottage was also where Darwin completed the final draft of *The Structure and Distribution of Coral Reefs* – one of the fruits of his voyage on the *Beagle* – and the birthplace of William Erasmus, the couple's firstborn. Altogether their union produced ten children, seven of whom survived into adulthood, with William becoming the subject of one of the earliest studies in what would now be termed developmental psychology.

Though by no means viewing the infant as a mere subject – Darwin clearly adored his new son and described him as 'a prodigy of beauty and intellect' – many hours were spent studying the child's behaviour, his facial expressions and mannerisms. A diary was kept for several years in which William's gestures and development were described in detail, comparisons being made between these observations and those Darwin had made in the orangutan enclosure at Regent's Park Zoo. At the time such a comparison of child and ape might have been considered quite scandalous, but Darwin's findings are known to have inspired several important European and American academic psychologists working in the early twentieth century.

Surprisingly, given his output and his lasting influence, Darwin was neither a dry academic nor a rampant workaholic. When invited to join the *Beagle* he had no scientific training whatsoever, although he was keen and reportedly adept at taxidermy. (Having already amassed large private collections of rocks, fossils, beetles and barnacles, he also knew what to look out for and how they should be classified once they were found.) Instead, for most of his life he rarely worked more than two hours at a stretch, and had to take frequent rests before returning to his labours. This was something of an irony for someone so closely associated with the notion of the survival of the fittest – but then to be fair to Darwin the phrase is not his, nor is there any evidence that he ever used it himself.

28. Lady Ottoline Morrell (1873-1938)

44 Bedford Square, WC1

Aside from some memoirs and a journal she chose not to publish, Lady Ottoline Morrell put neither pen to paper nor brush to canvas, yet as both patron and hostess became a key member of the Bloomsbury Group of writers and artists.

From 1906 celebrated soirées were held each Thursday at her home in Bedford Square, and later at 10 Gower Street when she and her politician husband fell on harder

BLOOMSBURY: LIVING IN SQUARES, LOVING IN TRIANGLES

Although her half-brother succeeded to the dukedom of Portland, the Morrells were never quite as rich as their artistic friends imagined, which may excuse those who took advantage of her largesse. There was also rather more to the couple's marriage than might have been assumed, with Philip Morrell's well-known philandering at times well-matched by that of his wife. Despite her voice and a face that was likened to that of a horse she was evidently sexually very attractive to many in her circle. Her lovers included D.H. Lawrence, the philosopher Bertrand Russell, and the artists Augustus John and Dora Carrington, although Vita Sackville-West found her 'a very queer personality ... with masses of purple hair, a deep voice, teeth like a piano keyboard and the most extraordinary assortment of clothes, hung with barbaric necklaces'.

times. The guest list was impressive at both (as it was at their country house, Garsington Manor in Oxfordshire), although the hostess was not infrequently ridiculed by many of her guests for her strange voice – 'a weird, nasal, cooing, sing-song drawl' – and a preference for wearing medieval and Renaissance costume. Nearly six feet tall and with a penchant for towering hats, the vivacious redhead was also caricatured in several novels, not always warmly, including Aldous Huxley's *Crome Yellow* (1921), *Women in*

Love (1920) by D.H. Lawrence and Graham Greene's *It's a Battlefield* (1934).

Lady Ottoline's simple desire was 'to live life on the same plane as poetry and as music' and throughout her life she sought to surround herself with like-minded souls. These included the aforementioned as well as poets W.B. Yeats, T.S. Eliot and Stephen Spender, young artists such as Mark Gertler, Stanley Spencer and his younger brother Gilbert, and the controversial sculptor Jacob Epstein.

Despite the ridicule – which mostly went on behind her back – Lady Ottoline was a popular and extremely well-intentioned individual. In the words of one of her protégés, 'passionate and ambitious and exceedingly observant and sensitive', she remained convinced that 'every penny one can save ought to be given to young artists', and always insisted that 'we who really feel the beauty and wonder of art ought to help them'.

The young, she felt, had 'such a terrible struggle' and besides buying many works of art herself from up-and-coming artists she worked hard to introduce them to rich friends who might do likewise. To others, such as the art historian Roger Fry, she gave substantial sums of money – sadly the pair later fell out due to his jealousy of Ottoline's long-running affair with Bertrand Russell – while Gilbert Spencer was given accommodation on the Morrells' country estate.

The Tudor manor at Garsington, built on land once owned by Geoffrey Chaucer, had been acquired in 1914 in a state of considerable disrepair. Once restored, and amidst what Lytton Strachey described as 'a surging mesh of pugs, peacocks and pianolas', it provided an important haven for Ottoline's artistic London friends. These included several seeking to avoid prosecution as conscientious objectors (by working on the land during the Great War), the Morrells having by this time become involved in the recently established Union of Democratic Control (UDC).

The UDC had three key objectives: the seeking of proper parliamentary control over foreign policy as a way of avoiding secret diplomacy; the formation after the war of an organization intended to prevent future conflicts; and the imposition of peace terms that would neither humiliate defeated nations nor artificially redraw national frontiers in such a fashion as to provide a cause for renewed fighting. Thus configured it rapidly acquired a membership of more than three hundred thousand in Britain but was perceived by others as anti-patriotic rather than anti-war – and even pro-German.

Before long the *Daily Express* was exhorting its readers to find out where UDC meetings were being held, and to break them up if necessary by using force. Complaints about this from UDC members went unheeded by both the Home Secretary and the Metropolitan Police, and the idea was allowed to develop that the organization – and those associated with it – were dangerous 'conchies'. In fact this was far from the case and, like Lady Ottoline herself, the UDC was very well intentioned if, ultimately, entirely unsuccessful in its objectives.

Garsington Manor was in any case always very much a cultural retreat rather than a political base, and over a period of more than ten years the visitors' book was graced by the likes of Leonard and Virginia Woolf, Siegfried Sassoon, Clive and Vanessa Bell, John Maynard Keynes, E.M. Forster, Ralph and Frances Partridge and Vita Sackville-West. But sadly by 1927 the same financial pressures that forced the move from Bedford Square to Gower Street meant Garsington had to go, and Britain's intellectual and artistic elite lost a uniquely special and valuable institution.

Unfortunately for Lady Ottoline things were to worsen dramatically from this point onwards. Within months she had been diagnosed with cancer of the jaw, the pain from which was indescribable and the damage appalling. Losing all her lower teeth and much of her jaw, she had afterwards to disguise her disfigurement by swathing her head in veils and scarves. For such a social figure it seemed an especially cruel blow, but at Gower Street the soirées slowly began again and continued into the late 1930s, when she suffered a devastating stroke. Treated with an untested drug – her physician subsequently killed himself – her condition rapidly worsened and on 21 April 1938 the colourful Lady Ottoline Morrell was pronounced dead.

29. Gunther Plüschow (1886-1931)

British Museum, Great Russell Street, WC1

With no address in London besides the great Bloomsbury institution where he spent the summer of 1915 lying low, Plüschow was a pioneering Bavarian aviator and explorer whose considerable achievements in life have been overshadowed by his escape from a prisoner-of-war camp in Leicestershire.

In truth his escape was not difficult, and both before and since countless German POWs managed to break out of their huts or climb over a few strands of barbed wire. What distinguishes Oberleutnant Plüschow, however, is that he made it back home from Britain, the only German POW to achieve this in either of the two world wars.

Plüschow had been captured in Gibraltar, but only after an extraordinary journey from China where he had shot down a Japanese aircraft with his pistol. After crashing in a rice paddy, and burning his Rumpler Taube to prevent the little monoplane falling into enemy hands, he had spent months travelling back to Europe. His journey had taken in Nanking, Shanghai, Nagasaki, Honolulu, San Francisco and New York, and for obvious reasons British Gibraltar had not been on the itinerary. It was Plüschow's misfortune that when the ship on which he was travelling ran into bad weather it had been forced into port.

Locked up in Leicestershire, he escaped within weeks of his arrival in Britain and made his way south to London. Despite police notices asking the public to look out for a foreigner with a dragon tattoo, he managed to escape detection for weeks on end. Spending his days at the docks – reasoning that a foreigner here was less likely to arouse suspicion – at night he would conceal himself among the famous mummies and marbles of the British Museum. Astonishingly he was even confident enough to have his picture taken at this time, but only after using coal dust and boot polish to dye his fair hair a greasy black and soot to darken his skin.

Wartime security meant that no notices were posted about vessels entering and leaving the Thames, but from a mysterious lady friend Plüschow learned of a ship, the *Princess Juliana*, which was leaving for the Netherlands. Sneaking aboard further downriver at Tilbury, within days he was back home in Germany and being greeted as a hero.

Because his death or recapture would have been such a propaganda gift to the kaiser's enemies, he was grounded for the remainder of the war. But in 1919 he regained his wings and resumed his travels, making several expeditions to South America before crashing fatally onto a glacier in Chile. London's reluctant guest was just forty-four years old when he died.

30. Bob Marley (1945-81)

34 Ridgmount Gardens, WC1

Having failed to establish himself outside Jamaica, the reggae singer struck gold when he was introduced to Chris Blackwell. The meeting took place at the Speakeasy Club, a notorious venue for musicians and music producers alike, where late-night drinking and good vibes were guaranteed.

A short walk from his Bloomsbury flat, the Speakeasy was the place at which Marley went on to perform his first-ever London gig. The club's manager at the time, Laurie O'Leary, despite his initial concerns over the musician's style, offered Marley a consecutive four-night slot, the only time such an offer was made to anyone. The applause soon drowned out any lingering fears O'Leary may have had about the popularity of Marley and his music.

Meeting Blackwell in London provided the kick Marley needed to start his international career. As owner of the independent Island Records company, and as one of the first to record Jamaican popular music, Blackwell went on to introduce Marley and the Wailers to a worldwide audience.

Over the years Marley moved around London, taking up residence in various parts of the city, including Mayfair and Chelsea (where he lived in exile following an assassination attempt in Jamaica) as well as Bayswater and the famous Rastafarian squat in Kennington's celebrated St Agnes Place.

Marley's widow, Rita Marley, says her husband had a special affinity with London, and it was clearly reciprocated with thousands of Londoners attending his shows. More recently a plaque has been affixed to 34 Ridgmount Gardens, stating that the 'Singer, Lyricist and Rastafarian Icon Lived Here, 1972'.

Chapter 7

FITZROVIA AND REGENT'S PARK

31. Lord Arthur Somerset (1851-1926)

19 Cleveland Street, W1

A great nineteenth-century *cause célèbre*, the Cleveland Street scandal of the summer of 1889 fuelled accusations many of which have still not entirely been laid to rest. It also encouraged a belief that still prevailed at the prosecution of Oscar Wilde a few years later, namely that homosexuality was on the whole an upper-class perversion in which innocent working-class youths were corrupted by aristocrats.*

---

* Reviewing Wilde's *The Picture of Dorian Gray* in 1890 one newspaper slyly described it as being suitable for 'none but outlawed noblemen and perverted telegraph boys'.

Almost by accident the affair came to light when a messenger boy working for the London Central Telegraph Office on the corner of Newgate Street and St Martin's Le Grand was found in possession of fourteen shillings (seventy pence). The sum aroused suspicion not simply because messengers were forbidden to carry their own money while working but because it was equivalent to several weeks' wages for a City messenger.

Facing an accusation of theft, the boy told the police he had come by the money while moonlighting as a prostitute in Cleveland Street. According to rumours circulating at the time he had lent weight to his alibi by identifying a brothel there and naming several of its socially more prominent customers. These were said to have included: Lord Arthur Somerset, a younger son of the 8th Duke of Beaufort and equerry to the Prince of Wales; the Prince's son, HRH Prince Albert Victor who was thus second in line to the throne; and Henry James FitzRoy, Earl of Euston.

At that time any homosexual act even between consenting men in private was a serious criminal offence, punishable by up to two years' imprisonment with hard labour. When Lord Euston's name was mentioned in the press in connection with such unsavoury goings on he decided to sue the newspaper in question for libel. He won, admitting only that he had visited the brothel but had left immediately he realized the nature of the place, thus forfeiting the sovereign he had paid to enter. Another of the accused, Lord Arthur Somerset, had meanwhile gone to Germany (but only after being interviewed twice by officers working on the case) and officially at least there was no word at all about His Royal Highness.

Lord Arthur's journey was not in itself suspicious as his destination was the fashionable spa at Bad Homburg where the Prince of Wales was taking the waters. In his absence, however, one of the rent boys admitted to police that Lord Arthur had paid him for sex, and two other minor players in the drama subsequently received rather modest sentences of just a few months apiece after pleading guilty.*

It also emerged that the brothel-keeper Charles Hammond had fled to the United States on a ticket apparently paid for by Lord Arthur, and that the legal costs of the two young men charged with prostitution had been settled in a similar manner. From this point on, the equerry made just two brief appearances on home soil – at a horse sale at Newmarket, and for his grandmother's funeral – before fleeing to France.

Clearly Somerset had been tipped off, and amidst much clamouring from journalists and others for action the Lord Chancellor, Lord Halsbury, seems to have blocked any attempt to bring the accused back to

---

* By comparison the editor found guilty of libelling Lord Euston was jailed for a year.

face justice. Prime Minister Lord Salisbury was similarly assumed to have decided that no moves should be made to extradite Hammond from the US, something that lent credence to the idea that what the Establishment really wanted was for the whole affair to be quietly dropped.

Many months later a warrant was finally issued for Lord Arthur's arrest, but almost certainly this was done only to appease public opinion as there was absolutely no chance now of it being served in France. The unusually lenient sentences handed down to the two youths also appear suspicious and were perhaps calculated as part of an effort to ensure that both went quietly rather than causing the scandal to blow up even further. It has more recently been alleged that the Prince of Wales wrote to the prime minister to thank him personally for allowing his equerry to escape, and had asked for assurances that if Lord Arthur ever did return to England he would not be arrested.

True or not, Lord Arthur chose to stay away and he seems to have lived comfortably in self-imposed exile before dying peacefully just shy of his seventy-fifth birthday. Even so, interest in the case has never quite gone away, with most of it naturally focused on the role supposedly played by the young royal. The truth is that no evidence of his involvement has ever come to light, nor indeed can it be said with any certainty that he was even gay or bisexual. But unfortunately the prince's death less than three years after police raided Cleveland Street has served only to fuel rumours that he was up to no good. More recently the idea has taken hold that his involvement in the scandal so outraged public opinion that the Establishment decided he should be bumped off, thereby removing him from the line of succession.

Needless to say, there is no substance to this, nor to the even more outlandish theory that the prince, perhaps driven mad by undiagnosed syphilis, was Jack the Ripper. The reality is that Albert Victor wasn't even in the country at the time London's East End was being terrorized, and his death at just twenty-eight was simply one of a million or more that resulted from the great influenza pandemic that swept Europe in the 1890s. Similarly, back in Cleveland Street, we also know that none of the defendants ever mentioned him by name, although to the conspiracy theorists such details never seem to matter.

In fact it now seems as though the whole thing leads back to Lord Arthur Somerset and his solicitor, Arthur Newton, who may have cooked up the whole thing in order to deflect attention from his client. If so, it was an audacious plan and an outrageous one for a man of the court to conceive. But it was also a plan that seems to have worked, and it would certainly not be the first time – nor the last – that a lawyer had taken money to lie. Of course this too may be impossible to prove now, but Newton certainly has form. In 1910 he was struck off for altering letters from another client, Dr Crippen, and in 1913 he was jailed for obtaining money by deception.

However he did it, with friends in high places or just one low one, at a time when his actions constituted a serious crime, Lord Arthur Somerset walked.

32. Sir Henry Wellcome (1853-1936)

6 Gloucester Gate, NW1

Britain has good cause to regret that the immense legacies of Andrew Carnegie and the little-known James Smithson favoured the United States,* but occasionally significant philanthropic flows can run in the opposite direction. It was an American banker, for example, who established the Peabody Trust in 1862 (which now has nearly twenty thousand affordable dwellings in London) and a Wisconsin-born pharmaceuticals magnate whose fortune lies behind one of the world's leading medical charities, the London-based Wellcome Trust.

Back in Wisconsin, Henry Solomon Wellcome had shown himself to be something of an entrepreneur from

---

* The will of this illegitimate son of the 1st Duke of Northumberland stipulated that should the male line of his family fail his considerable fortune was to be used to found an educational institution – the Smithsonian – in Washington, DC.

a young age, and as a teenager was already selling ordinary lemon juice to be used as invisible ink. By 1880 he was in London in partnership with another American, the pair establishing themselves in the pharmaceuticals business under the name Burroughs Wellcome & Co. Silas Burroughs had trained as a pharmacist, but Wellcome had the complementary marketing flair and introduced a new kind of compressed pill or tablet, which was quickly trademarked under the name 'Tabloid'. Another of his innovations was to talk directly to doctors, offering them free samples in the hope that paid orders would follow.

The ploy worked, and when Burroughs died in 1895 Wellcome found himself in sole charge of a large and complex yet immensely profitable network of companies headquartered in Snow Hill, Holborn. From now on the profits were carefully ploughed back into the business, establishing world-class research laboratories, a popular Historical Medical Museum (which opened just before the Great War at 54a Wigmore Street) and a Wellcome Institute that included significant teaching facilities within its Academic Unit. The business expanded internationally but the focus was always on London, Wellcome becoming a British citizen in 1910 and basing himself at Gloucester Gate from 1920 until his death.

Inevitably, home life took second place to Wellcome's ballooning business interests. According to his biographer, the large house was neither luxurious nor somewhere he chose to spend much time, and while his marriage to fashionable interior decorator Syrie Barnardo produced a child it cannot be judged a success. Wellcome eventually divorced her, naming the writer William Somerset Maugham as co-respondent. (The pair married – equally disastrously* – but in fact the cuckolded Wellcome could have named several others instead, including department-store owner Harry Selfridge.)

The details surrounding the Wellcome/Barnardo divorce generated acres of press coverage, none of it pleasing to the plaintiff. In response, the already private man became a reclusive one, Wellcome from then on choosing to pour his considerable energies into the accumulation on his own account of immense collections of medical artefacts and books on related subjects.

With a lifelong passion for anthropology Wellcome's stated intention had always been to establish a Museum of Man in London, and by 1920 the expansion of his collection had displaced the pharmaceuticals company as his primary interest in life. Employing a global network of agents and dealers to buy on his behalf, this was soon said numerically to be five times larger than that of the Louvre in Paris. To prevent prices rocketing to artificial levels Wellcome shrewdly decided to buy anonymously,

---

* Maugham was predominantly homosexual, and married Syrie Wellcome only after the birth of their daughter became public knowledge.

SO MANY THINGS,
BUT WHERE TO SHOW THEM?

Buying on such a scale it was perhaps inevitable that only
a small proportion could ever be displayed, and in fact
during Wellcome's lifetime it is likely that no more than
one in ten of his prized artefacts ever saw the light of
day. It is doubtful too that his private anthropological
museum could ever have accommodated the entirety of
a collection had his plans ever come to fruition. Indeed,
thought to have numbered around 1.5 million objects by
the time of his death, Wellcome's personal hoard would
have dwarfed many of today's national collections.

pay cash for all purchases and despatch unmarked vans
to collect the goods.

Such buying strategies demonstrate that Wellcome
clearly knew what he was up to, and that his enthusiasm
was by no means the sort of uncontrolled mania sometimes exhibited by other collectors operating on a similar
scale. His agents were always given very clear instructions
as to what to buy (and how much to pay) and they would
have recognized that their client was spending many
hours a day personally identifying specimens and select-
ing those he wished to purchase.

Nor should Sir Henry, who was knighted in 1932, be
considered a failure simply because his great dream of
a great museum foundered. Today, remarkably, almost

everything he created more than a hundred years ago
still exists, much of it scattered and now operating under
other names, but much of it enriching the cultural, academic and professional lives of many tens of thousands
of Londoners as well as visitors to this great city.

The pharmaceutical company has gone: it was sold
off in the 1990s and now forms part of the international
giant GSK (GlaxoSmithKline). But the contents of the
old historical medical museum are on permanent loan to
the Science Museum, its award-winning Wellcome Wing
(built using funds provided by the Wellcome Trust) now
one of the most popular in terms of visitor numbers.

Sir Henry's vast library similarly forms the basis of the
Wellcome Library, with more than half a million volumes
devoted to the history of medicine, while the six hundred
thousand images housed in the Wellcome Trust Medical
Photographic Library place it among the most important
resources of its kind anywhere in the world. As for the
aforementioned Academic Unit of the old Wellcome
Institute, that too has survived and is now an integral
part of University College London.

It perhaps goes without saying that, like the Science
Museum extension, the trust established on Sir Henry's
death has also paid for the buildings from which
these organizations now operate. But even that's not
all. Charged not just with maintaining and expanding
its founder's collections but with funding biomedical

research in London, the Wellcome Trust continues to do so to the tune of more than £600 million annually. Saving lives as well as enriching lives, after so many years Henry Wellcome's legacy is extraordinary.

33. Virginia Woolf (1882-1941)

29 Fitzroy Square, W1

Aged fifty-nine when she donned an old overcoat, filled the pockets with stones and wandered out into the cold waters of the River Ouse in Sussex, the sad lonely death of one of the Bloomsbury Group's central figures continues to haunt readers and scholars after more than seventy years.*

Woolf had frequently complained about the noise in London; she chose to end her life in the country, and more than once she expressed a wish that 'Bloomsbury was on the seashore' – but she remains a quintessentially London figure even while her ashes lie a few miles from Lewes at

---

* That it took three weeks for the body to be found adds to the horror, so too the note she left for her husband Leonard: in it she wrote, 'Dearest, I feel certain that I am going mad again. I feel we can't go through another of those terrible times. And I shan't recover this time. I begin to hear voices, and I can't concentrate. So I am doing what seems the best thing to do.'

Rodmell. Born in Kensington to an upper-middle-class family, raised in a house in Hyde Park Gate, and educated at King's College London, when she moved out of the parental home it was to Fitzrovia. The house in Fitzroy Square had previously been occupied by George Bernard Shaw, and when she left there it was for a larger house in nearby Brunswick Square and then another in Gordon Square.

This first place she shared with her younger brother Adrian Stephen who later made his name as an author and Freudian psychoanalyst. Both of them were convinced they were now living in penury, and there was much talk of tripe and tinned fish. But while Fitzrovia lacked the social tone of Mayfair and Belgravia there was clearly plenty of family money to pay servants to look after them in their bohemian redoubt.

Woolf's first actual earnings had been for a commission from the *Times Literary Supplement* to write about the Brontës in Yorkshire, but journal entries from this period describe her taking in London spectacles too. These included the annual Royal Academy Reception, at which 'trains disgorge hundreds of thousands of fair ladies elegantly attired', and a trip on a fairground ride at Earl's Court. Here she and Adrian 'floated along a kind of drain which is worked by electricity so that the current floats you without oars [through] grottos & sunsets & effects of light upon water'. She was unimpressed by this, thinking it 'a horrid fraud', but they returned each year for another go.

Later diary entries describe her unease at the cheers that went up when a Zeppelin was brought down, killing the crew, and the strangeness of the capital during the General Strike in 1926. Armoured cars were to be seen driving up and down Oxford Street and, in the absence of any public transportation, 'everyone is bicycling'. With

A LIFE LIVED, AND NOW STUDIED

From the earliest years Virginia Woolf was emotionally a very troubled individual, something that has made her a fascinating subject for those studying literature and mental illness. Losing her mother and a half-sister while still a teenager, and being institutionalized several times after the death of her father in 1904, there is also a suggestion that she and her sister (the painter Vanessa Bell) were abused by their half-brothers George and Gerald Duckworth. This did not prevent Woolf from seeking the latter's assistance when it came to the publication of her early novels, but has provided contemporary literary scholars with another rich vein of enquiry in addition to the more conventional evaluation of her importance as a feminist and pioneering English modernist writer.

no one working she found 'one of the curious effects ... is that it is difficult to remember the day of the week'. And when, finally, the strike ended on 11 May, Woolf observed a policeman on duty smoking a cigarette, a sight 'I dare say I shall never see again; & don't in the least want to'.

Woolf's first novel, *The Voyage Out*, was begun at the house in Fitzroy Square, in a second-floor room, although publication was delayed until 1915. By this time her mood swings were becoming more erratic and she had already spent at least three spells at Burley House in Twickenham, a place politely described as a 'private nursing home for women with nervous disorders'. Despite these interruptions she managed to continue writing through most of the emotional chaos, many of the resulting volumes being published by the Hogarth Press, which she founded in 1917 with her husband Leonard Woolf.

From the start their marriage was a complex organism even by Bloomsbury standards. Aside from the usual affairs – Virginia had a particularly passionate interlude with the snobbish Vita Sackville-West – there was the issue of Leonard's religion. In common with much British writing at this time, her portrayal of Jews in her novels was unsympathetic and frequently grotesque. More bizarrely she complained in her diaries how much 'I do not like the Jewish voice; I do not like the Jewish laugh' and even admitted how much she had 'hated marrying a Jew' – and, worse still, 'a penniless Jew'.

Theirs was, even so, one of the happier liaisons in their social circle, and one of the most productive with the Hogarth Press commissioning work from prominent Bloomsbury figures including fellow anti-Semite T.S. Eliot as well as outsiders such as Sigmund Freud and Laurens van der Post.

The union was also to provide the single most positive and nurturing influence on Virginia's life, Leonard devoting much time and effort to her care. The last words she wrote recognized this – 'You have given me the greatest possible happiness. You have been in every way all that anyone could be. I don't think two people could have been happier' – and when his own time came in 1968 he determined that his ashes should join hers at Rodmell. This he did even though much of the intervening quarter of a century had been spent in the arms of his lover, 'Trekkie' Parsons.

34. Dylan Thomas (1914-53)

Fitzroy Tavern, 16 Charlotte Street, W1

Dylan Marlais Thomas mostly spent only odd spells in London – often dossing down with the poet Louis MacNeice in Islington – and there is scant evidence that any of his poetry was written in the capital. His name nevertheless frequently surfaces in conversations about literary London during and after the Second World War (particularly when they relate to Fitzrovia) despite as one biographer put it his being merely 'a commuter – writing in Wales and travelling up to London to drink'.

The poet's wife Caitlin, a dancer, was also a drunk and similarly destructive – Thomas described their marriage as 'raw, red bleeding meat' – and the two lived a largely peripatetic existence between London, Wales, Oxford, Ireland, Italy and New York. They moved into a cottage in Laugharne paid for by the wife of the historian A.J.P. Taylor, and a Blue Plaque in Delancey Street, NW1 indicates a brief stay in a basement flat that was also owned by Taylor. But the building most closely associated with the Welshman is, appropriately enough, a pub on Charlotte Street where it is possible that the pair first met in the late 1930s.

The Fitzroy Tavern is also what gives this area of north Soho its name, the term 'Fitzrovia' having first appeared in print in 1940 in the gossipy William Hickey column in the *Daily Express*. The author was Labour grandee and KGB double agent Tom Driberg MP, although it is likely that he was simply repeating a term used by one of the pub's regulars, the artist Augustus John. The tavern in turn took its name from the original landowners, the FitzRoys, the family of the present Duke of Grafton.

FITZROVIA BECOMES BOHEMIA

One of four surviving dukedoms to be descended from the bastards of Charles II, the FitzRoys developed much of this area, which they owned from the 1720s to the 1920s. As such they are commemorated in several street names and nearby Euston Station is named after Euston Hall, the Suffolk home of the present Duke of Grafton.

With the exception of the eponymous square, however, it was never a particularly smart or fashionable suburb, and as the rich gradually migrated west once-elegant terraces were subdivided into flats, artists' studios and workshops. From the late nineteenth century onwards, writers and other impecunious sorts began flooding into the area, the likes of George Bernard Shaw and Walter Sickert – as well as Thomas and his circle – cementing its reputation as a seedy yet lively and at times genuinely creative bohemian nexus.

Either at the Fitzroy or the Wheatsheaf in nearby Rathbone Place, Thomas made a drunken proposal of marriage to Caitlin and, once accepted, the two were reportedly in bed within ten minutes. Marrying in Cornwall, and settling in Laugharne, they returned to London in 1941 – leaving their son with his grandmother – where Thomas hoped to join the wartime Ministry of Information as a film-maker. Many writers found employment here – including Graham Greene,

J.B. Priestley and George Orwell – but Thomas was rejected before being taken on by Strand Films, an independent contractor.

As it was to be for most of his life, Thomas's existence was more or less hand-to-mouth, and he revelled in his reputation as a drunk and ultimately doomed artist. In this regard there were many others like him, pubs such as the Fitzroy, Wheatsheaf and York Minster being where they preferred to gather. Here, according to one publican, 'if one of them sold a picture, or had an article accepted, they were all in the money for as long as it lasted. Then they were all broke until another one was lucky.'

Thomas had hoped to supplement his meagre income by writing begging letters to more successful literary figures, but the plan failed. Despite his reputation the war years were not entirely wasted, however, and during this period he completed several scripts for the BBC, and five more that were eventually filmed by Strand as patriotic pieces of propaganda.

It was also for the BBC that Thomas penned his 'infernally eternally unfinished play' – *Under Milk Wood*. This most enduring classic had begun life as a short story called *Quite Early One Morning*, which was produced for radio in 1945. Unfortunately *Under Milk Wood*'s gestation was so long that by the time of its debut broadcast in January 1954 its author was already three months dead.

Albeit posthumously it made his name, and it is inarguably his greatest work. That it took so long to complete was not entirely down to the poet's famously dilatory nature, however, but rather to the fact that the author lost no fewer than three manuscript versions before it could be produced.

The first went missing after a reading in Cardiff, the second at the Poetry Centre in New York. On the third and most famous occasion he mislaid a completed draft while on a visit to another favourite haunt, the aforementioned York Minster in Dean Street.* Fortunately this last one resurfaced pretty quickly – Thomas had simply put it under his chair and several hours later staggered off into the night without it – but it was later the subject of a legal case when his widow failed to prove ownership.

The fateful trip to Soho had taken place on 18 October 1953, and though no one knew it at the time it was to be the poet's last 'commute'. The following morning Dylan Thomas left for New York and three weeks later he was dead. The cause was alcohol-related pneumonia and he was thirty-nine years old.

---

* Better known as The French House, the pub where Brendan Behan is said to have written *The Quare Fellow* formally adopted its longstanding nickname in 1984. This was a reference to a former licensee – actually a Belgian – who took over the pub during the Great War. His son, Gaston Berlemont, was born in the pub in 1914 and was still running it seventy-five years later.

35. Guy the Gorilla (c.1946–78)

Zoological Society of London, Regent's Park, NW1

A western lowland gorilla captured in French Cameroon, and the oldest in Europe at the time of his death during a routine dental extraction, Guy was for decades one of London Zoo's biggest attractions. He made numerous television appearances as well as being the subject of the popular 'A Life in the Day' column in the *Sunday Times*, and a lifesize bronze sculpture of him can still be seen by visitors to Regent's Park.

For many the ideal celebrity in that he never spoke and spent his life locked in a cage, Guy was by no means the zoo's first big draw. A hundred years earlier visitor numbers had literally doubled when Londoners flocked to see Obaysch, Europe's first hippo since Roman times; and, before being sold to P.T. Barnum, Jumbo the elephant had been so popular that thousands of children had written to Queen Victoria in the hope of keeping him in London.* Then there was A.A. Milne's son Christopher Robin who named his teddy bear Winnie after Winnipeg,

---

* The American circus owner paid the zoo $10,000, or about £150,000 in today's terms.

a Canadian black bear that had been donated to the zoo in 1914, and in 1949 the first polar bear ever bred in Britain attracted three million visitors in a single year, a figure that has yet to be surpassed.

For all that, however, there was always something a bit special about this gorilla. A truly formidable beast with a seven-foot chest measurement, as a baby he had arrived from Paris on Guy Fawkes Night 1947, hence the name. Traded for a rare tiger he was first photographed clutching a hot-water bottle against the November chill, and cowering at the sound of nearby fireworks. As far as the public was concerned it was love at first sight, and the love never failed. In the absence of an accurate date, the zoo arbitrarily decided the young ape's birthday was 30 May, and from then on Britain's largest and most famous primate received hundreds of cards annually until his death decades later.

Largely passive, the giant silverback had occasional bursts of temper, and would sometimes throw his 530-pound bulk against the reinforced glass that fronted his palatial three-room enclosure. At other times, however, he was seen to scoop up carefully small birds that had flown into his cage, examining them closely in his immense hands before releasing them to fly off.

Whilst most of the press immediately labelled him a gentle giant, his portrayal in the *Sunday Times* as something of an old curmudgeon – 'I don't go in for all this friendship stuff with human beings, not like stupid chimps' – seemed only to add to his appeal. Perhaps the biggest regret is that he never bred, although attempts were made to interest him in a female called Lomie beginning in 1969.

His sudden death from a heart attack was a genuinely sad blow to staff and his regular visitors, not least because by this time he had been a fixture of the place for more than thirty years. In the wild Guy might have been expected to live to forty, and examples in zoos have survived to fifty. Unfortunately, a post-mortem revealed that Guy had become clinically obese, almost certainly due in part to his daily intake of ice cream and dozens of sweets before the zoo took steps in 1968 to prevent visitors from feeding the animals.

In one sense at least Guy was to live on, however. While sculptor William Timym worked on the aforementioned bronze for the zoo, the taxidermy department at the Museum of Natural History was charged with preserving the original. It took nine months in all, the slow and painstaking work of the museum's chief taxidermist, but in 1982 beautifully modelled and mounted Guy went on display in South Kensington. It is true that not everyone applauded Arthur Hayward's work – some people just don't like stuffed animals – but at the time of writing Guy has taken up position in the museum's prestigious Cadogan Gallery.

As part of a permanent collection entitled 'Treasures' he joins a rare first edition of Darwin's *Origin*, a genuine piece of moon rock and a stunning nautilus shell from the famed collections of Sir Hans Sloane.

Chapter 8

KENSINGTON AND CHELSEA

36. Lord Leighton (1830-96)

12 Holland Park Road, W14

As the home of the first artist in this country to be knighted, the first to be given a baronetcy and the first to be raised to the peerage, Kensington's Leighton House Museum opened in 1929 and is one of London's most unexpected and delightful.

A Grade II* listed building by the architect George Aitchison, the artist's former home has been compared to a geode, being exceptionally plain without but a polychromatic palace of glitter and elaboration once its portal has been breached. When it was completed in

1879 Leighton himself described it as his autobiography, and certainly it is hard to think of another building that better describes the wealth, taste and high social standing of a prominent and successful artist at the peak of the Victorian era.

Frederick Leighton moved to the south of England as a young man (from Scarborough) and was educated at University College London. His was an unusually well-travelled family – one of his grandfathers had been court physician to two tsars – and the impressively multilingual Leighton spent time in Germany, Italy and France mingling with artists such as Ingres, Corot and Louis Gallait and improving his technique at academies in Berlin, Frankfurt and Florence. Very much the defining period of his younger life, the experience nevertheless brought on bouts of depression and was the beginning of lifelong concerns about his eyesight.

By the age of twenty-five he had completed his first major work, *Cimabue's Madonna Carried in Procession through the Streets of Florence*, the sale of which (to Queen Victoria for an astonishing six hundred guineas) ensured a reputation that having soared into the firmament never quite returned to earth. A few years later he was said to be earning as much as £4,000 annually, a figure at least a hundred times in excess of the national average, the prices for his paintings quickly doubling and trebling as they passed from one collector to another.

THE FIRST AND LAST
LORD LEIGHTON

Leighton's well-deserved peerage is now remembered as the shortest-lived in British armorial history. The letters patent creating the barony Leighton of Stretton were signed on 24 January 1896 but the recipient died the following day of angina pectoris. Unmarried and without issue, the prized baronetcy 'of Holland Park Road in the Parish of St Mary Abbots, Kensington, in the County of Middlesex' was extinguished at the same moment. He was an intensely private man, more at ease with children than adults, and rumours still persist of at least one illegitimate child. These are, however, no louder and certainly no easier to prove than the rival assertion that as a bachelor the celebrated painter and sculptor was homosexual.

Leighton continued to travel through Europe, the Middle East and North Africa but soon settled permanently in London. Here he associated with many leading figures of the Pre-Raphaelite Brotherhood, although he did not identify at all with many of their ideas. He also found himself at the centre of a unique artistic enclave as other successful figures, including G.F. Watts, Luke Fildes, William Holman Hunt and Marcus Stone, began commissioning their own houses-with-studios around the corner from his.

Leighton described the resulting loose-knit community centred on Melbury Road as a mews, but this was entirely disingenuous. These were and are still immense detached houses of very considerable quality, as good as (if not better than) any in the area. Designed by such luminaries as Halsey Ricardo and Richard Norman Shaw (William Burges naturally designed his own) they illustrate perfectly the wealth and respectability of a new generation of artists who formed a decidedly un-bohemian caste. Only Leighton's friend Lawrence Alma-Tadema seemed able to resist the attraction of the area, choosing to remain in St John's Wood where his vast, domed palace – much extended after its purchase from the French artist James Tissot – can still be seen in Grove End Road.

Leighton's choice of architect is interesting too, in that it mirrors and proclaims his own rise to the very summit of the artistic establishment. Just as Aitchison was to become president of the Royal Institution of British Architects, Leighton had assumed the presidency of the Royal Academy as well as being given the command of the Artists Rifles, an extremely well-regarded London regiment that still exists as part of the SAS Reserve.

This important military role, along with a profusion of honorary doctorates and Leighton's seat on the boards of the British Museum and National Portrait Gallery say much about his acceptance into the upper echelons of society and his impressive administrative abilities. They also explain James McNeill Whistler's sardonic comment that he 'paints a little too, I believe', although this is possibly apocryphal. Either way Leighton took understandable pride in his advancement, and a self-portrait for the Uffizi shows the artist in all his glory, depicted in academic garb that shows the gold seal of the Royal Academy, which the painting just fails to obscure. In the background is part of the British Museum's Parthenon frieze, a replica of which Leighton had commissioned for his own studio.

Throughout his life Leighton's most successful works harked back to the same classical period, although as a Victorian he was able to imbue these with a certain sentimentality. For these his models included Ada Pullan and her sisters, members of a large family living nearby who supported themselves for many years by sitting for Leighton and others in the Melbury Road set.

Known professionally as Dorothy Dene (she had some success on the stage) Ada Pullan's flawless complexion, abundant chestnut hair and classical figure conformed very closely to Leighton's physical ideal and she appears in several of his later works, including the celebrated *Flaming June* and as one of the *Greek Girls Playing at Ball*. Ada is also the probable prototype for the character of Eliza Doolittle in George Bernard Shaw's *Pygmalion*, as Shaw was good friends with Leighton and his muse at the time he was writing the play. She died in 1899, aged just forty-four, and was laid to rest à la mode in the stylish cemetery at Kensal Green.

Although ill-health forced Leighton's father to retire early he had survived into his ninety-fourth year, but once again his was an example not followed by his son. The artist had been diagnosed with angina in his fifties but chose to maintain his usual hectic schedule of work, travel and countless civic responsibilities. In 1895, ignoring a further diagnosis of serious exhaustion, he returned to North Africa and Italy but by New Year – when the hitherto unheard of privilege of a peerage was gazetted – he was clearly in poor shape. He never recovered and on 25 January he died peacefully in this wonderful house, surrounded by family and friends. A little over a week later he was interred in St Paul's Cathedral, final proof were it needed that the Establishment was burying one of its own.

37. Duleep Singh (1838-93)

53 Holland Park, W11

Conceivably the first Sikh to settle in Britain, the story of the last native ruler of the Punjab is a uniquely melancholy tale of personal dislocation, political intrigue and imperial manoeuvring.

In 1843, as a child of five, Singh had been declared Maharajah of the Sikh Empire following a series of battles and skirmishes in which every other claimant to the throne had been either killed or murdered. With the throne came a fabulous but ill-fated diamond, the 108 carat Koh-i-Noor, which was said to carry an ancient curse that can be avoided only when the stone is in the possession of a woman.

Politically Singh's position was never better than tenuous, and indeed by the age of eleven he found himself deprived of the throne. Defeat in the Second Anglo-Sikh War saw control of his empire pass to the ferociously expansionist directors of the Honourable East India Company in March 1849. Within months the young maharajah was spirited away and isolated from his family, and in order to sabotage any attempt to restore his rule the decision was taken to Anglicize him as quickly and as thoroughly as possible.

By 1853 Singh was living in London, initially in a suite at Claridge's before more suitable accommodation was provided for him by the East India Company at Roehampton. Evidently very fond of the handsome young man, Queen Victoria invited him to visit her at Osborne House on the Isle of Wight, the Prince Consort commissioned a new coat of arms for him, and Singh found himself fêted by English society. But while fully engaged initially, he eventually tired of such a life and

FROM A GOLDEN THRONE
TO GOLDEN HANDCUFFS

Controversially the young boy was more or less com-
pelled to convert to Christianity, and in exchange for
a British government pension of £50,000 a year to
renounce any claim to the throne. In 1850, as a further
humiliation, now a maharajah in name only, Singh was
required to travel to London personally to present the
Koh-i-Noor to Queen Victoria. Although Her Majesty
was not yet Empress of India, the potent symbolism of
the ceremony must have been plain to all.* More than
once it was also made clear to Singh that the generous
pension was conditional on his continuing obedience to
the wishes of the British government, and that he was
forbidden to return to India.

---

* The slight has never quite been forgotten, and as recently as
2002 a spokesman for the Indian High Commission in London
stated that his government had a legitimate claim on the diamond
and that this would be forcefully renewed.

after undertaking an extensive tour of Europe Singh set
himself up as a country gentleman on the seventeen-
thousand-acre Elveden Hall estate in Suffolk.

Acquired on his behalf by the India Office, the hall
was expensively remodelled in an extraordinary and lavish
oriental style, and gaining a reputation as one of the
dozen best shots in the country Singh was soon a regular
guest alongside the Prince of Wales at great shoots such as

Highclere Castle and Blenheim Palace. Notwithstanding a failed and ruinously expensive attempt to breed his own red grouse, Elveden was successfully transformed into one of the best shooting estates in the country and at Grandtully in Perthshire he held the record for the number of grouse shot in one day.

Marriage to the Cairo-born Bamba Müller in time produced six children, two of whom became known affectionately as the Black Princes. Both were fine shots and after following the well-trodden path of Eton and Cambridge joined the British Army. But behind the picturesque image the former maharajah was becoming restless and dissatisfied. Faced with mounting money problems, in 1881 the Singhs were forced to leave Elveden and return to London, the debt-laden estate subsequently being sold to the Earl of Iveagh, head of the Guinness brewing family.

Singh's intention was now to live at No. 53 Holland Park 'with my family and as economically as possible'. For five years he attempted to do no more than this, but in 1886 when the government refused to increase his pension or to return the Koh-i-Noor his mood blackened. Leaving his family in Holland Park, and dismissing his erstwhile friend the Queen as a 'Mrs Fagin', Singh decided to return to India to reclaim his birthright.

He had been allowed to visit only once before, to bury his mother; but even this had been a highly controversial proposition and her body was kept at Kensal Green Cemetery for almost a year while the authorities debated how to manage things. When finally allowed to travel he was carefully chaperoned but this time they were taking no chances. No reasonable attempt could be made to prevent an ostensibly free man from leaving the country but, amid concerns that he was planning to raise a revolt among his former subjects in the Punjab, Singh was apprehended in Aden. On the orders of the Governor-General of India he was placed under arrest.

Having returned to his old faith while in the colony, and now required to return to Europe, on his release Singh instead travelled to tsarist Russia. As an old antagonist of the British Empire it was hoped that St Petersburg could be persuaded to support his cause, but when no help was forthcoming he travelled to Paris. Suddenly a broken man, Duleep Singh chose to settle in the French capital rather than returning to his family in London.

His wife died the following year and although No. 53 stayed in the family until 1890 Singh was never to see London again – nor indeed India. Three years later he too was dead, aged just fifty-five, but even then he was denied a last chance to go home. With the authorities at home and on the subcontinent still fearful of the symbolic value of a well-attended public funeral, Singh's body was brought back to England and interred in the little churchyard at Elveden alongside that of his wife.

Disgracefully, the quiet funeral was conducted according to Church of England rites and done so in the full knowledge that the deceased had publicly abjured Christianity during his brief stopover in Aden. Once more the message was clear to everyone: just as in life he had been a hapless pawn in a high-stakes game of intrigue and ambition so now the last maharajah's final wish was to be sacrificed to political expediency.

38. The Ghost of Lillie Langtry
(1853–1929)

Cadogan Hotel, Pont Street, SW1

Famed as 'the Jersey Lily' after the island of her birth – and immortalized in a song by The Who more than a century later – in 1877 Emilie Charlotte Le Breton* became famous almost overnight, after being invited to a soirée by society hostess Lady Sebright.

At that time, married to a dim but reasonably rich Irish drunk, Lillie had nothing but pale golden hair, good looks and charm. The presence of several artists at the Sebrights' that night was to change all that, however,

---

* By no means certain is the claim that she is descended from Richard le Breton, one of the four knights believed to have murdered Thomas Becket in 1170.

ensuring that news of her beauty spread throughout a significant strand of London society. Thereafter, having sat for several of her fellow guests, including John Everett Millais, Edward Burne-Jones and Frank Miles, her fame was assured once a painting of her had been acquired by Prince Leopold, Duke of Albany.

Queen Victoria's fourth and youngest son was to die prematurely (of haemophilia) but his interest in Lillie proved contagious and as she recalled in later life, 'from that time I was invited everywhere and made a great deal of by many members of the royal family and nobility'. Shortly afterwards she took to the stage, at the suggestion of Oscar Wilde, a close friend and later her Chelsea neighbour. But it is for her love life that Lillie is now best remembered, in particular for an affair with Leopold's eldest brother 'Bertie', the future Edward VII.

Her acting career was even so by no means unsuccessful. More popular with audiences than with critics, she starred in several West End productions, toured the US a number of times and for three years leased and managed the Imperial Theatre in Westminster (on the site of what is now Methodist Central Hall). In later life she bred race horses, and settled in the

United States where she established a successful winery, but in the public imagination the association is always made with her lovers rather than anything she herself managed to achieve.

As a mistress she must have been remarkable, managing somehow to establish and maintain a cordial relationship with the future king's wife Princess Alexandra (who almost from the start knew what was going on) and even being presented to his mother, the queen.

For a while Bertie was clearly besotted, famously entertaining her in one of the private rooms at Rules (a second door to the Covent Garden restaurant is still said to have been installed so that the couple could enter and leave without being observed) and building a hideaway for them both in Bournemouth, which is now run as the Langtry Manor Hotel.

In all, the affair lasted a little over two years, by which time Bertie had moved on (possibly to another actress, Sarah Bernhardt) as had Lillie. In 1879 she was being seen increasingly in the company of the Earl of Shrewsbury and with Prince Louis of Battenberg. The latter had apparently been encouraged in this by Bertie himself when rumours began to circulate that Edward Langtry was thinking of divorcing his wife and threatening to name the Prince of Wales in court.

The following year she found she was pregnant, and with some confusion as to who was the father Prince

Louis was sent off to sea – appropriately enough on board the HMS *Inconstant* – while Lillie, still married, disappeared to Paris. Here she was delivered of a daughter, Jeanne Marie. (On finding out as an adult that she was illegitimate and not liking it, Jeanne Marie was reportedly ticked off by her mother who asked whether she would rather be the daughter of a drunken Irishman or of a prince.)

In the event, the child's paternity was not proven, but her existence was more than enough for Langtry who finally divorced Lillie and went on his way. By now the two had been living apart for several years, Lillie moving first to a house in Dunraven Street in Mayfair and afterwards to 21 Pont Street, an imposing terracotta structure that now forms part of Cadogan Hotel.* Though it was to remain her home for no more than five years – after taking American citizenship she retired to Monaco – she returned to the hotel many times, always staying in the same suite of rooms. When she died in 1929, aged seventy-five, she was buried on Jersey alongside her parents in St Saviour.

Happily today there is still something of her in London, as to the delight of many guests her ghost is said to walk through her old rooms, which are now used for private

---

* Coincidentally it was in Room 118 of this same hotel that Lillie's old friend Oscar Wilde was arrested and charged with committing acts of gross indecency after the collapse of his foolish libel action against the 9th Marquess of Queensberry.

dining. Apparently she makes only rare appearances, preferring to appear only when the hotel is relatively empty, making her seem a somewhat more retiring figure than her reputation might lead one to suppose – and enigmatic to the end.

39. Krystyna Skarbek (1908-52)

1 Lexham Gardens, W8

Widely touted as the model for one and possibly two Bond girls, this Polish-born agent of Britain's Special Operations Executive (SOE) was awarded the Croix de Guerre as well as the George Medal. She survived the war but died in tragic circumstances a few years later, after being stabbed by a stalker in the lobby of a cheap London hotel.

Distantly related to the composer Chopin, as 'Christine Granville' Skarbek was one of the earliest recruits to SOE and was thus among Britain's longest-serving wartime female secret agents. Serving Britain to liberate her own country, her initial contact was with MI6, the Secret Intelligence Service, on whose behalf she returned to occupied Poland. There she helped to establish a network of covert observers and couriers charged with acquiring useful intelligence about the enemy and transmitting it to London.*

Soon active in Hungary, Skarbek showed her talent for the kind of courage and quick-thinking improvisation on which the life of a good agent often depends. Captured and interrogated by the Gestapo, she bit down hard on her tongue knowing that if she began to cough up blood it would appear that she was suffering from TB. The ruse worked and, fearful of contracting the disease, the interrogating officer quickly released her.

Travelling by way of Turkey and Cairo, Skarbek eventually found herself in France, a replacement for another female operative who had been captured and imprisoned. Despite the obvious risk to herself, she attempted to obtain the release of two other agents who had been captured by the Gestapo, Christian Sorensen and the British author Xan Fielding. She did this by posing as the niece of British Field Marshal Montgomery, assuring the senior officer in charge that if he executed the men she would personally ensure that his name was added to a list of Nazis who would likely be prosecuted at the war's end.

As an added inducement she offered a bribe in return for the men's safety and once again, and not less surprisingly, her ploy worked. After many hours haggling the two

---

* This included a working example of an advanced new Polish-designed anti-tank gun used by the Axis Powers, which Skarbek concealed in her apartment.

THE SPY PIONEER

Once recruited into the newly formed SOE – the organization that at its inception in 1940 was famously ordered by Winston Churchill to 'set Europe ablaze' – Skarbek's effectiveness and undoubted success are thought to have been key in the pioneering decision to recruit more female agents. Making an invaluable contribution to the vital work of SOE, these were to include several whose names subsequently became very well known, including Violette Szabo (a sometime resident of Stockwell), Vera Atkins, Odette Sansom and Noor Inayat Khan.

men were set free, with Skarbek only later realizing the enormity of the risks she had taken and that she could well have found herself joining Sorensen and Fielding at the wrong end of a firing squad. Instead the three found themselves on the road to safety, subsequently learning that at the war's end the bribed officer had been murdered, presumably by the French Resistance although this is not known.

Skarbek's exploits were certainly recognized at the time, and indeed she was one of very few SOE agents to reach the rank of captain. However, with the war finally won her star quickly waned, and depressingly she found herself entirely unable to secure the kind of work where her unusual skills might have been useful. It was around this time that she is rumoured to have had an affair with the dashing Commander Ian Fleming of British Naval Intelligence (hence the suggestion that when he turned to writing he used her as the model for two characters, Vesper Lynd and Tatiana Romanova), but with no country to return to and just a month's salary in lieu of notice she was soon out of the service and forced into a variety of low-paid menial roles.

These included stints working as a housekeeper and as a shop assistant and by 1952 she was working as a stewardess on a cruise ship. More glamorous than most (not least because the captain insisted she wear her medals) she caught the eye of a cabin attendant, Dennis Muldowney. She rejected his advances but he misunderstood and when the two went on leave that June he tracked her down to her digs at the Shelbourne Hotel in Kensington.

In particular Muldowney took the greatest exception to her plan to visit a former lover and fellow SOE agent, the Polish war hero Andrzej Kowerski. Becoming more agitated he eventually pulled out a knife and a struggle ensued in the lobby of the hotel with the night porter rushing to intervene after hearing Skarbek's plea to 'Get him off me!'

Tragically, by the time the two were separated Skarbek was already dead from a deep chest wound. Muldowney immediately admitted that he had stabbed her, but blamed his victim for leading him on. Describing her as a 'modern pimpernel no man could resist', he admitted his guilt again when the police arrived to take him away, telling the arresting officer 'I built all my dreams around her, but she was playing me for a fool.' Pleading guilty at the Old Bailey a few months later he was sentenced to death within three minutes of entering the dock. His trial is still the shortest on record, and at Pentonville on 30 September while insisting that 'to kill is the final possession' he took the drop.

Krystyna Skarbek's death at the age of just forty-four was squalid and tragic, and all the more so given the much greater dangers she is known repeatedly to have faced while in the service of her adopted country. Unsurprisingly the story captured the imagination of the press and public, and for a few weeks she was rightly hailed as a heroine, albeit a dead one. Of course had her story been more widely known before that night in the hotel, she would not have been a ship's steward, never met Muldowney and in all likelihood never have entered the hotel.

But of course she was and fatefully she did, and it is here in London that she died after years spent dodging death in occupied Europe. At least as 'Christine Granville' she enjoys some measure of immortality, in that no history of the Special Operations Executive can ever be complete without a detailed record of her extraordinary achievements. Similarly she lives on as the prototype for a certain kind of Bond girl, in the pages of *Casino Royale* and *From Russia with Love*. Xan Fielding too acknowledged his debt to her in the dedication to his book *Hide and Seek* and in the pains he took to document her courage and the multiple injustices of her end.

As to an actual memorial, ahead of Muldowney's execution she was laid to rest beneath a tall cross at St Mary's Roman Catholic Cemetery in north-west London. In 1988 she was joined by the ashes of Andrzej Kowerski, and as her tomb is rarely if ever without flowers it seems safe to assume that the courage and talents that once were overlooked are recognized at last.

Chapter 9

SOUTHWARK AND THE SOUTH BANK

40. John Tradescant (c.1570-1638) and John Tradescant (1608-62)

St Mary-at-Lambeth, Lambeth Palace Road, SE1

These days the name John Tradescant can usually be relied upon to ring a bell among those who know London, although many forget that there are two of them: father and son.

Keen gardeners both, and even keener hoarders of much that was weird or wonderful, they helped kickstart a national obsession that encompasses everything from the sweeping landscapes of Brown and Repton to the tiniest inner-city window box.

The fragrant lilac, the acacia tree, Kew Gardens' celebrated yellow double daffodil, the ubiquitous London plane tree, and several edible fruits we now take for granted (including the pineapple and the apricot) are just a few of the species brought to these shores by the Tradescants.

John the father originally cut his teeth as an explorer, visiting the Russian Arctic in the company of the splendidly named gentleman-adventurer Sir Dudley Digges. It was whilst they were fighting Algerian pirates in the 1620s that Tradescant discovered the apricot, and around this time too that he started laying out formal gardens for the nobility and later King James I.

Turret Grove, his wonderfully eccentric south London home, was popularly known as Tradescant's Ark for its immense collections of diverse beasts and birds, fishes, shells, fossils and stones. When he died John the son took over, adding yet more bizarre items to his father's collection.

These included a stuffed dodo from Mauritius, something Tradescant insisted was 'a natural dragon, above two inches long' and a sample of blood said to have 'rained down on the Isle of Wight'. A deer skin and shell cape belonging to the father of Pocahontas sat alongside a 'brazen ball ... to warm the Nunnes hand' and the remains of the lantern Guy Fawkes was said to have been holding when he was captured.

Members of London society soon beat a path to his door to see such treasures and by the time he died the Ark, by now renamed the Musaeum Tradescantianum, was recognized as the finest collection of its kind. As such it attracted the attention of one Elias Ashmole who, as crafty as any lawyer and determined to get his hands on Tradescant's rarities, moved in on his widow.

His ruse worked and soon twelve cartloads of curiosities, very much London's loss and Oxford's gain, were assembled as the core of the Ashmolean Museum. Many of these original curiosities can still be seen amidst the more than three hundred thousand exhibits that make up the world's oldest public museum. However, it took a few hundred years for the Tradescants to get the memorial they deserved in the city they called home.

That memorial is the Museum of Garden History, based on the south bank of the Thames at the redundant church of St Mary-at-Lambeth. Besides regular exhibitions on gardening and related matters, and a re-creation of a seventeenth-century knot garden by the Dowager Marchioness of Salisbury, the church is home to the wonderful Tradescant family vault, a veritable riot of strangeness entirely in keeping with the extraordinary addictions of the two Johns.

Beneath a lid of black marble is a sarcophagus decorated with exotic carvings of ancient Greek buildings and Egyptian pyramids, broken classical marble columns, sinister crocodiles pushing their snouts up through the primeval gloop, an obelisk, small carved trees at each corner and at one end a truly hideous many-headed hydra picking at a skull. They have company too – Captain Bligh of the Bounty was buried next door in 1817 and there are at least two Archbishops of Canterbury for neighbours, one of whom controversially read the sermon at the funeral of Nell Gwyn; also a generous benefactor called Bryan Turberville who left the parish £100 in 1711, but on condition that none of it was ever given to chimney sweeps, fishermen or Roman Catholics.

41. Annie Besant (1847-1933)

39 Colby Road, SE19 *

A prominent early socialist and women's rights campaigner, Besant was born into a wealthy city family but after separating from her husband, a Lincolnshire vicar, she relocated to a Victorian semi in Southwark. Her choice, she wrote in her 1893 autobiography, was

---

* Besant was born in Clapham, and lived in a number of other houses in Hampstead, Paddington and St John's Wood, but as these have all now been demolished a commemorative Blue Plaque was affixed to the Gipsy Hill house in 1963. In her lifetime it would have been No. 26 Colby Road.

between 'hypocrisy or expulsion', and having lost her Christian faith in the early years of her marriage the twenty-seven-year-old housewife and mother unhesitatingly chose the latter. Her determination notwithstanding, she remained Mrs Besant for the remainder of her life, divorce at this time being not just something that was frowned upon but an expensive luxury for all but the upper-middle classes.

Her good fortune on moving south was to find herself among friends and fellow freethinkers, one of whom introduced her to Charles Bradlaugh, the founder of the National Secular Society (NSS). Besant found Bradlaugh's zeal and iconoclasm hugely appealing, and within weeks she was writing for the society's newsletter, the *National Reformer*, and considering taking up lecturing.

Annie Besant's first public talk was delivered very shortly afterwards, on the contentious issue of women's non-existent political status. It was well received and from that day the die seemed cast: the speaker had found her first cause, and in Annie Besant an important cause found itself a powerful advocate.

In quick succession she found herself drawn into the struggle for many associated freedoms, including birth control and workers' rights. The NSS was prosecuted in 1877 for publishing a controversial pamphlet on the first of these, specifically for promulgating material 'likely to deprave or corrupt those whose minds are open to

THE NATIONAL SECULAR SOCIETY

The organization founded by Charles Bradlaugh still exists today and from its base in Red Lion Square, WC1 continues to campaign against belief in the supernatural and to 'challenge religious privilege'.

Notable successes have included the repeal of ancient laws against blaspheming, but after nearly 150 years the society still campaigns to secure the disestablishment of the Church of England, withdraw public funding from religious schools – of all denominations – cancel any tax exemptions for churches, and end state-funded chaplaincies in prisons, hospitals and the armed forces.

Whilst not all of these campaigns enjoy particularly wide support it is important to note that the NSS is not anti-religion. Rather, in the best traditions of free thought, its members maintain that belief should be a private matter that belongs not in the public sphere but in the home or a place of worship. Today they include numerous Members of Parliament, Sir Jonathan Miller, Professor Richard Dawkins, Jonathan Meades and the popular television historian David Starkey.

immoral influences'. Besant was found guilty and imprisoned for six months, but the sentence was quickly overturned by the Court of Appeal.

As well as sitting on the board that first introduced free school meals in London, Besant was also a prime mover in the famous London matchgirls' strike in the summer of 1888. This involved as many as 1,400 workers employed by matchmakers Bryant and May, and was a protest against their woeful pay rates, a punishing work regimen of up to fourteen hours a day and the appalling health risks associated with the white phosphorus used in the factory at Bow.

Besant made several speeches outside the factory, and Bradlaugh, by this time MP for Northampton, raised the issue in the House of Commons. Galvanized into action by the bad publicity that the strike generated, the firm eventually backed down and accepted almost all the girls' demands. Even so, and despite the hideous effects of 'phossy jaw' (whose victims' bones actually glowed in the dark), deadly white phosphorus remained in use until the early twentieth century.

Surprisingly, given her back story and hitherto firm convictions, it was shortly after the successful conclusion of the strike that Besant underwent a religious conversion. First Anglican then atheist, following a meeting with the Russian mystic and occultist Helena Petrovna Blavatsky, Besant adopted the teachings of Blavatsky's Theosophical Society, established in 1875 for the 'study and elucidation of Occultism, the Kabbala etc.' and based in what is now the British Medical Assocation's Bloomsbury HQ.

Besant continued writing and talking but increasingly it was on behalf of the Theosophical Movement as her interest in secular and secularist matters declined. Subject to many schisms, despite a founding principle based on a belief in the universal brotherhood of humanity, her new enthusiasm took its name from the Greek *theos* (god) and *sophia* (wisdom). Much of its teachings had their origins in Eastern philosophy, and in due course Besant left London for Madras on the Indian subcontinent, where she lived for most of her remaining forty years.

Eventually assuming the presidency of the Theosophical Society, Besant had her reforming zeal rekindled in India. Besides founding a groundbreaking school for boys called the Central Hindu College, she joined the Indian National Congress (INC) and began campaigning for Indian home rule. Not yet a call for full independence, this new movement gained power and influence at the outbreak of the Great War. A call for the British Empire to support the war in Europe encouraged a belief that 'England's Need is India's Opportunity', and the fact of her arrest and internment in 1917 says all that needs to be said about Besant's growing influence.

In the face of protests over her imprisonment, from Hindus and Muslims alike, Besant was freed shortly afterwards. She was then briefly president of the INC, although it is to be assumed that the irony of an English woman holding such a post was not lost on many. Shortly after the defeat of Germany the leadership of the struggle for home rule and then full independence was taken over by Mohandas Gandhi and Besant's fellow theosophist

Jawaharlal Nehru.* Besant disagreed with much of the new politics but continued to support their desire to leave the British Empire, and after her death at Adyar in 1933 her ashes were scattered on the Ganges River rather than being returned home to London.

42. 'Sax Rohmer' (1883–1959)

51 Herne Hill, SE24

The evocative pen name of Arthur Henry Ward, Sax Rohmer was the creator of one of fiction's most durable criminal masterminds in the evil persona of Dr Fu Manchu. A Birmingham-born journalist, Ward moved to Herne Hill in 1910 and remained there until 1919 when ballooning royalties and the fact that his marriage was childless made possible a move to a smaller but decidedly smarter address in Bruton Street, Mayfair.

As a jobbing wordsmith Ward's early work had been diverse and included a spell producing fresh material for two giants of the London musical hall, Harry Relph (aka

---

* Both future leaders were sometime residents of London, with official Blue Plaques for Gandhi at 20 Baron's Court Road, W14 and for Nehru at 60 Elgin Crescent, W11. Curiously the first governor-general of an independent Pakistan, Muhammad Ali Jinnah, was the former's near-neighbour when he lived at 35 Russell Road, W14.

'Little Tich') and George Robey.* Long interested in the occult, he also claimed membership of a number of cults, including the Rosicrucians and the intriguingly named Hermetic Order of the Golden Dawn. Membership of the latter is thought to have included a number of writers, including Arnold Bennett, E. Nesbit, Bram Stoker and (less surprisingly) Aleister Crowley – but like Ward's own membership this is not readily proven.

Gradually a developing interest in Egyptology began to colour Ward's attempts at short story writing, and his first published story was *The Mysterious Mummy* in 1903. It was a switch to the Orient a decade later that really propelled Ward into the ranks of the bestsellers, however, and prompted him to adopt his most celebrated nom de plume.

Making his first outing in *The Mystery of Dr Fu Manchu* the evil genius from the East caught the public's imagination immediately and more than a dozen sequels appeared, several of which were written in Herne Hill. Most offer a somewhat challenging prospect for the modern reader – the depiction of many of the characters is frequently so stereotypical as to be offensive – but perhaps no more so than the writings of 'Sapper' and Erskine Childers and even some of John Buchan's output.

---

* Even before he came to London Ward/Rohmer had good vaudevillian connections and in 1909 married a variety-hall artiste called Rose Elizabeth Knox. A juggler whose brother Teddy was a member of the original Crazy Gang, she too eventually turned to novel writing.

Serialized over many months, the stories introduced readers to the machinations of the 'Yellow Peril'. This globe-striding conspiracy pitched expert poisoner and dastardly schemer Manchu against his nemesis Sir Denis Nayland Smith, late of Scotland Yard. The two were to meet many times over the coming years with the tall, lean 'sun-baked' Sir Denis always emerging the victor. The first instalment included a breathless chase from the opium dens of crime-ridden Limehouse, east London through various of the country houses of England, providing a recipe that the public both here and in the US seemed slow to tire of.

A sociologist has since pointed out that, at the time of the book's publication, the Limehouse Chinese community was actually one of London's more law-abiding ethnic minorities. But realism was never the point and as Rohmer scribbled away his creation grew like Topsy, making countless appearances in comic strips and songs, on radio and in cinemas where, on occasion, he has been portrayed by Lewisham's own William Pratt – or as movie-goers know him, Boris Karloff.

Like Arthur Conan Doyle the author was eventually exhausted by his money-spinning creation, and dropped him; but as with Holmes the public clamour forced a return.

More than a decade after the first Fu Manchu stories another instalment duly appeared, the series eventually running on for nearly half a century. It ended only with Rohmer's own death in 1959, when he was cut down by a bout of Asian flu, which some might consider an example of poetic justice.

Between Fu Manchu's various outings Rohmer experimented with a mixture of other protagonists, including an 'occult detective' as well as several conventional ones. These too met with success – with or without the Yellow Peril his name sold books – and for twenty years prior to the Second World War Rohmer was to be counted among the world's highest-paid authors. For some of these he returned to Chinatown – most famously to write *The Mystery of the Shrivelled Hand* – but other novels and short stories explored similarly exotic Islamic themes together with house-hauntings, more traditional supernatural horrors and that other perennial favourite of readers, the mad scientist.

Despite the acclaim and the move to Mayfair, Rohmer's private life was dogged by intermittent money worries, although more as a consequence of mismanagement and poor investments than extravagance or bad habits. In later life some relief from this came in the form of his final creation, Sumuru, a sort of female Fu Manchu. She was created in response to a BBC request for a character to star in a radio series for broadcast on the Light Programme. In place of the Yellow Peril listeners were chilled by the equally sinister Order of Our Lady, and once again the mix proved such a hit that the first eight episodes were fashioned into a new novel.

This too did extremely well – particularly in the US where it was retitled *Nude in Mink* – and in short order it was followed by four sequels. Two of these were filmed in the 1960s, with Shirley Eaton in the title role, the same star who appeared alongside Christopher Lee in *The Blood of Fu Manchu*. Like that one, neither was anything but a harmless piece of hokum, but with the doctor making his final cinematic appearance as recently as 2007 – so far anyway[*] – there is no doubting the power and endurance of Herne Hill's most famous son.

43. Sir Alan Cobham (1894-1973)

78 Denman Road, SE15

Just shy of Alan Cobham's tenth birthday the Wright Brothers managed to stay aloft for just twelve seconds, yet such was the pace of progress in the world of aviation during his lifespan that by the time of Cobham's death twelve men had actually walked on the moon.

---

[*] Nicolas Cage made a brief cameo appearance as an openly camp Fu Manchu in a spoof trailer for *Werewolf Women of the SS* (2007) by 'Rob Zombie'.

For that game-changing first 'sustained and controlled heavier-than-air powered flight' at Kitty Hawk Sands, Orville Wright travelled just 120 feet – less than the wing-span of a modern passenger jet. But within six years Louis Blériot had flown from one side of the English Channel to the other, and earning his wings young Cobham soon began to envisage crossing continents.

The son of a Camberwell tailor, Cobham had been educated at a local grammar school with seventeenth-century origins. Soon an interest in geography developed into what he later described as a romance.* Wartime service as a pilot with the Royal Flying Corps provided the opportunity to see things from a new perspective, and by the war's end Cobham had become a passionate advocate of powered flight.

If ever there was a perfect moment for aviation to take off, this was it – and within very few years the dream of a new world linked by air was well on its way to becoming a commercial reality. Among hundreds of demobbed avia-tors, men like Cobham led the charge, their exploits and dash bringing glamour to this exciting new technology. With the public flocking in huge numbers to airshows at Hendon and a score of wartime airfields, demonstration flights gave thousands of ordinary Britons their first taste of the future. Typically a 'five bob flip' took approximately

* Wilson's School still exists and in 1975 relocated to the site of the old Croydon Aerodrome.

RIGHT PLACE, RIGHT TIME. RIGHT MAN, RIGHT STUFF

Cobham's timing was fortuitous to say the least. Britain alone had constructed more than 5,500 flying machines during the Great War and with the hostilities finally brought to a close the authorities in Whitehall were keen to offload hundreds of surplus biplanes at genuine bargain prices. Typically in Britain this was done by placing advertisements in the new specialist press, magazines such as *The Aeroplane*, where a typical insertion might read 'For Sale. Avro 504K in perfect working order. £40'.

fifteen minutes once the pilot's wife had collected the fee (twenty-five pence).

Cobham had a much larger vision, however, and while employed by the De Havilland company at Hatfield he undertook a series of longer and longer flights. These were mostly around Europe and the Mediterranean, and then in 1926 he announced his intention to fly one of the company's frail DH-50s from Rochester in Kent to London's Westminster Pier. His plan was to take in Australia along the way, a journey that took him three months and cost the life of his engineer when the poor fellow was shot by a startled Bedouin tribesman somewhere over the desert.

Upon his return from the far side of the globe Sir Alan

flew the now badly battered DH-50 up the Thames as far as Hammersmith before banking round and turning back over Westminster Bridge to land on the water outside the Palace of Westminster. The crowds lining the bridge were ecstatic, the feat earning Cobham a knighthood and, more importantly, convincing the normally conservative authorities that, with such a vast empire to service, men like this might hold the key.

So far commercial flights had been fairly modest affairs: the first from London to Le Bourget carried only one passenger (who paid £21 for the privilege), along with some grouse, a few pots of Devonshire clotted cream and a selection of daily newspapers. But Cobham's exploits encouraged the government to take matters in hand and, looking for a way to link the far-flung corners of the British Empire, Sir Alan and fellow south Londoner Air Vice-Marshal Sir Sefton Brancker, chairman of the Royal Aero Club, were asked to establish a viable air route to India for Britain's first national airline, Imperial Airways.

Today, though perilous in the extreme, such an exercise sounds impossibly romantic. The splendidly named Imperial Desert Air Mail Service, for instance, flew from Cairo to Basra via Gaza and Baghdad, a small fleet of archaic wooden biplanes offering passengers a connection along the way (from an airstrip hidden among Mesopotamian sand dunes) to take them up to Lake Tiberias then on to Athens and Genoa in northern Italy.

Even more remarkable was the London–Singapore–Brisbane route that was announced in late 1934. This journey took an astonishing twelve days end-to-end, but then outright speed was really of little consequence when the only alternative was a sea voyage that could take literally months.

With a rather frivolous signpost at the entrance to London's Croydon Aerodrome – Cairo 2,000 miles; Karachi 4,000 miles; Johannesburg 6,000 miles; Sydney 11,000 miles; and so on – the success of many of these new long-haul routes depended on Britain's fabulous Empire C-Class aircraft. With room for seventeen passengers and five crew, these immense silver flying boats were the most luxurious machines of their day and could put down almost anywhere. For example, taking off from Lake Victoria they had a runway the length of Ireland to play with, an arrangement that avoided all the paraphernalia and expense of planning, earth-moving and civil engineering required to translate field and forest into a viable commercial airfield.

Even flying boats could run out of fuel, however, but again Sir Alan was quickly on the case. (Being Alan Cobham, he once admitted, was 'a full time job'.) Exhausted by crossing continents, but understandably reluctant to spend his time giving joy rides at airshows, instead he established a number of aviation companies. These included the aircraft manufacturer Airspeed, where one of his fellow directors was the bestselling novelist Nevil Shute. (The pioneering aviatrix Amy Johnson was an early subscriber to its shares.) Another was formed to develop the kind of in-flight refuelling systems on which modern air forces depend.

The idea was far from straightforward, relying on slightly Heath Robinson arrangements of pipes and grappling hooks being manipulated by pilots who were both steady and skilled fliers. However, the principle was good and, using an experimental single-engined Airspeed Courier refuelled by a much larger Handley Page biplane, Sir Alan became the first man to fly non-stop from England to India.

Soon his company, Flight Refuelling Ltd, was able to provide the means for more than a dozen non-stop transatlantic crossings by C-Class flying boats. Further development was curtailed by the outbreak of a new war with Germany, but it resumed in the 1940s with Sir Alan still in harness. He eventually retired to the Virgin Islands but returned to Britain, an old man by the 1970s, and died at home in Bournemouth. The company still exists today under the name Cobham plc.

Chapter 10

FURTHER AFIELD

44. Peter the Great (1672-1725)

Sayes Court Street, SE8

With the experience of the Cold War behind us, not
to mention mysterious deaths such as those of Georgi
Markov and Alexander Litvinenko, you have to go back
a very long way to find a top-ranking Russian whom
the authorities in London were happy to have poking
around – even longer when this took place within the
walls of a strategically important defence establishment.

In 1698 the extraordinary happened, however, when
Tsar Peter the Great arrived in London. He was the first
Russian tsar to leave his country in peacetime, and at war
with either Turkey or Sweden for much of his reign was

keen to find a way for his country to compete with Europe in terms of its fighting technology. He took a particular interest in maritime matters, and was keen to discover as much as he could about shipbuilding in general and, more particularly, to understand what lay behind Britain's growing naval supremacy.

Officially the trip was supposed to be made incognito, which would have been difficult as the Russian ruler was conspicuously tall at six feet seven inches. Being a keen sailor he also had unusually calloused hands for a sovereign. In any event 'Peter Mikhailov' was recognized immediately at many of the places he visited during his four months in the capital, and is known to have conducted a considerable amount of business while collecting thousands of pounds in bribes and inducements from merchants and financiers wishing to trade with Russia upon his return.

This last factor, indeed, goes a long way towards explaining Peter's presence in London, as the king, William III, was among those leading the drive to open up trade with the Russian Empire. In particular there was a desire to sell tobacco to the Russians, which Britain was at this time importing in abundance from its colony of Virginia.

For much of what Peter called his 'Grand Embassy' he was holed up in Deptford where he and his retinue had taken over Sayes Court, the diarist John Evelyn's country house. This suited his purposes admirably, the house

RUSSIA'S
ROYAL WRECKERS

A senior member of Charles II's court, and sometime treasurer of Chelsea Hospital, John Evelyn let his eighteen-room mansion to Admiral John Benbow who in turn sublet it to the visiting tsar.

This turned out to be a huge mistake and before long Evelyn's steward was writing to his master complaining about the 'right nasty' people who made up Peter's large party of hangers-on. The floors and carpets, he said, were left stained with grease and ink, and the paintings looked as if they had been used for shooting practice. Many stoves, doors, windows and locks had been smashed, and no fewer than fifty chairs had disappeared completely, probably up in smoke after being used as kindling. Meanwhile, outside in the gardens that Evelyn had nurtured for forty-five years, more than four hundred feet of decorative holly hedging had been knocked flat during a game in which the Russians liked to push each other around at speed in wheelbarrows.

With so many of his possessions 'broke, lost or destroyed' Evelyn complained to the authorities and Sir Christopher Wren was asked to survey the damage. He found Sayes Court 'entirely ruined' – it was subsequently demolished and today much of the site is occupied by council housing – and Evelyn was compensated to the tune of just over £350, equivalent today to more than £650,000.

being well away from filthy, overcrowded London. It was also very convenient for the three months he spent studying ships' plans and working as a journeyman-shipwright or carpenter in the nearby King's Yard, the great naval dockyard established by Henry VIII.

While Peter's retinue did their worst at Sayes Court he made the most of his time, visiting the Royal Arsenal at Woolwich and the Royal Observatory at Greenwich, where he saw Venus with the first Astronomer Royal John Flamsteed. As well as attending meetings of the Royal Society, and making a trip to the Tower of London to observe the workings of Newton's Royal Mint,* he was seen at the Friends' Meeting House in Deptford in conversation with William Penn. For relaxation he patronized several taverns in the City of London, one of which in Great Tower Street (now gone) was subsequently renamed the Czar of Muscovy.

On a personal level, Peter's time in London was highly inspirational and it was to have an immediate and direct influence on the history of Russia from then on. Observing Western ways convinced Peter that European culture was superior to his own, a realization that led to many sweeping changes, including the relocation of his capital from Moscow to his new city of St Petersburg.

---

* The Constable of the Tower refused to show him the axe used to decapitate Charles I as he was worried that Peter might recall how angry the beheading had made his father – and thus throw the offending article into the Thames.

At the same time, what he saw in the gun foundry at the armoury, at the observatory and in the King's Yard led to huge advances being made in all aspects of Russian artillery, navigation and shipbuilding.

Armed with this knowledge Peter the Great was able to establish Russia's first proper navy, much of it based on British know-how, thanks to the more than sixty master shipbuilders and assistants, mast makers, riggers, joiners, anchor makers, captains, pilots, gunners and engineers who took up his invitation to quit London and travel back with him. By the time of his death around twenty-eight thousand sailors were serving on board forty-nine warships and as many as eight hundred smaller vessels, and from an industrial and imperial standpoint the country had been transformed into a genuine world power. The great tsar's grand embassy to London may have lasted just four months, but its impact has continued to be felt through the centuries.

45. William Hogarth (1697–1764)

Hogarth House, Hogarth Lane, W4

The painter and engraver is most closely associated with suburban Chiswick, an area that in his day lay well to the west of the city. He was nevertheless a quintessential London character, born at Smithfield (in Bartholomew Close) and dying after a vomiting fit in Leicester Fields at the home of his wife's cousin.* Between times he created a body of work that is at once accessible, complex and intensely detailed, as amusing as it is instructive, and as popular today as it was when it left his studio.

His popularity is perhaps best demonstrated by the size of his country retreat at Chiswick, which is both exceptionally large and very handsome. Also by the naming of a 1735 Act of Parliament that was passed in an attempt to protect the copyright of picture engravers. This was known to one and all (and still is) as 'Hogarth's Act' in recognition of the fact that among all London's artists he lost more money than anyone else as a result of works being widely plagiarized and sold at a discount. Albeit posthumously he is also the only artist to have a roundabout named after him, one of the more unexpected landmarks that the A4 incorporates as it makes its way out of west London.

Three years prior to the passing of Hogarth's Act his satirical work *A Harlot's Progress* had been the first of a succession of moralizing tales told in a sequence of six prints, an innovation that quickly caught on. It was followed by others in a similar vein, including *The Rake's Progress, Marriage A-la-Mode* and *Industry and Idleness* – all

---

* Neither property has survived, hence the lack of a Blue Plaque at either of these central locations.

194

of which sold in huge volumes. (In print form, that is. An attempt to auction the originals of *Marriage* ended in failure with only a single bidder at £120, whereas Hogarth had expected five times the sum.)

For subscribers at the time each saga had an entertaining but dense and complex story to tell about contemporary mores, and today – like single-image prints such as *Beer Street* and *Gin Lane* – they provide us with a detailed and compelling glimpse of what life was like in eighteenth-century London. Sadly, not all of the original paintings have survived – those for *Harlot* were destroyed in a country house fire in 1755 – but the full *Rake* sequence of eight can be seen at Sir John Soane's Museum in Lincoln's Inn Fields.

Technically expert, blessed with what one might now call a photographic memory for detail, success for Hogarth came relatively early and, despite his uncompromising stance when it came to painting what he saw, he was much sought after as a society portraitist and later succeeded his father-in-law as sergeant-painter to George II.

Hogarth was also something of a *bon vivant* – a bit of a dandy, he was a great drinker – but always took his work extremely seriously. Acknowledging his good fortune in having a unique facility for 'retaining in my mind's eye, without coldly copying it on the spot, whatever I intend to imitate', he had a social conscience that he used to good effect in the aforementioned *Beer Street* and *Gin Lane*.

MORE A REALIST THAN A DIPLOMAT

While personally generous and highly charity-minded –
favourite causes included orphanages and hospitals –
Hogarth could be aggressive and opinionated. He also
hated foreigners, especially the French, and was notori-
ously short with difficult customers. One of his sitters, a
particularly ugly aristocrat, refused to pay for his portrait
because he found the finished picture insulting. Most
artists, given such a commission, would have modified
the painting to disguise any imperfections, but Hogarth
refused and instead threatened to sell it to a freak show
after adding a tail and various other offensive append-
ages. The nobleman paid up immediately, but after
taking the picture home reportedly burned it.

The two prints were created to address something
that had become a major problem in parts of London
as a result of careless legislative changes introduced
by William III. In a bid to lure Londoners away from
imported spirits, gin had become effectively unlicensed
and was rarely if ever taxed. By the 1730s it was on sale on
every street corner, from an estimated fifteen thousand
outlets at its peak, and consumption that was already high
more than doubled in the course of a decade.

Uncomfortably aware that drinking on this scale
encouraged not just drunkenness but also idleness and
vice, Hogarth – who himself preferred wine and beer – was

persuaded by the Bow Street magistrate and novelist Henry Fielding to produce a work contrasting the delights of beer with the iniquitous perils of hard liquor. Looking at the two prints today it is easy to see how he achieved this, *Beer Street* depicting a cheerfully bucolic scene while *Gin Lane* explores the seedy and degrading downward path of anyone who succumbs to 'mother's ruin'.

This time Hogarth's focus was on London's working classes – the city's servants, apprentices and labourers rather than the more prosperous targets of *Rake* and *Harlot* – and today it is this broad sweep as much as anything else that explains the enduring appeal of his work. Fairgoers in Southwark, a family struggling through a performance at Sadler's Wells, cockfighting gamblers, an orgy of drinking at an unnamed tavern – more than any artist before or since, this one captured and catalogued our city in the round. From babes in arms to an execution at Tyburn, of Hogarth's London it can truly be said that all of life is here.

46. George Hodgson (?-c.1810)

Bow Bridge, London E3

Today IPA or India Pale Ale is perhaps most closely associated with the Suffolk brewer Greene King. However, its origins are to be found in east London, although beer experts and enthusiasts will happily spend hours arguing over a pint as to exactly who created this singular beverage.

The most commonly cited name is that of George Hodgson. His date of birth is unknown but by the 1750s he was running the Bow Brewery, close to the point where the River Lea was bridged in the early twelfth century. The crossing was built under the orders of Matilda of Scotland, Henry I's queen, who commissioned a distinctive bow or arched bridge linking Essex, London and Middlesex. This is said to have given the surrounding area its name.

In Hodgson's day a popular drink in the capital was porter, a type of dark brown, hoppy beer. In hotter climates, however, paler beers were thought preferable, although these had to be rather more heavily hopped in order to survive the journey. Such refreshment particularly appealed to officers and box-wallahs who left porter to enlisted men and the servant classes and were prepared to pay a premium for a superior pint.

Keen to profit from these increased margins, Hodgson was only one of many London brewers experimenting with this new sort of recipe, and he had the advantage of location over many of his rivals. Unlike theirs, his new beer was readily transported by barge down the Lea to East Indiamen waiting on the Thames. He was also shrewd enough to offer their captains extended periods of credit, enabling them to travel to the subcontinent, sell the stuff and then sail back again before having even to think about settling Hodgson's bill. Typically eighteen months' credit was offered at a time when a round trip was rarely completed in less than ten.

This turned out to be such a smart move that today Hodgson is widely lauded as the inventor of India Pale Ale. In all probability he never was, but once his name was set to music – you too can sing along below – his reputation was assured:

> *Who has not tasted of Hodgson's pale beer*
> *With its flavour the finest that hops ever gave?*
> *It drives away sadness, it banishes fear,*
> *And imparts a glad feeling of joy to the grave.*
> *O! to drink it at morning, when just from our bed*
> *We rise unrefreshed, and to breakfast sit down,*
> *The froth-crested brimmer we raise to our head,*
> *And in swigging off Hodgson, our sorrows we drown.*

47. Laura Bell (1829-94)

Woodbine Cottage, Fortune Green Lane, West Hampstead (now the site of Lyncroft Gardens, NW6)

Laura Bell was a notorious Antrim-born prostitute who is reputed to have been paid the equivalent of £250,000 in today's terms for spending a single night with Jung Bahadur Rana, the prime minister of Nepal.

A firm friend of the British, and a formidable ruler of Nepal, Rana's normally close focus on matters of state began to wander while on a trip to London. Described as athletic and handsome, and a skilled diplomat, Rana arrived in London with a huge cask of holy water from the Ganges for his daily ablutions. Eager to maintain the image of a pious man, and aware that in crossing the water he was – according to ancient Hindu tradition – risking social status, Rana insisted that the trip was vital to cement relations between the two nations. He was, he said, determined to meet with Queen Victoria but would return home immediately afterwards.

This apparently admirable objective quickly changed when he came into contact with the pulchritudinous Bell at a banquet given by the Honourable East India Company. Her small doll-like face, strawberries-and-cream complexion and cascades of glorious golden hair were more than he could resist.

A former Regent Street shop girl, the twenty-one-year-old Bell was already used to receiving the attentions of successful men. Oscar Wilde's father was an early client, but the affair with Rana proceeded on altogether much grander lines. Very soon she was gifted a large house in Wilton Crescent, along with hampers of rich clothes and a seemingly endless succession of jewels. The affair, even so, was to be short-lived. Within three months Rana returned home, reportedly to his lasting regret, where the memories of his warm relations with Miss Bell may have played some small part in ensuring Nepalese support for the British authorities in the 1857 Indian Mutiny.

Bell's life, meanwhile, took an extraordinary turn after her marriage to Augustus Frederick Thistlethwayte, the brother of another former client. The marriage was not a success: she ran up huge debts that the young army officer could not support, and there were to be no children. But then, quite suddenly, she announced that she had become a Methodist.

Determined to become a lay preacher, Bell began entertaining lavishly at the couple's home at 15 Grosvenor Square. The guest list for her dinners was exclusively male and, with her husband deigning only very rarely to attend, those present tended to be politicians and other influential public figures. Before long her preaching took her far beyond London and, still cutting a beautiful and glamorous figure, her meetings in Scotland were particularly well attended.

Controversy was never far away, however, and the huge body of correspondence that survives between Bell and William Ewart Gladstone continues to be the subject of salacious speculation. At the same time, the Thistlethwaytes were pursued through the courts for debt – a significant embarrassment to them socially, especially when it became apparent that for many years she had been making large and extravagant gifts to the politician.

To Gladstone's credit he made repeated attempts to refuse or return these. Several of his letters also see him advising her on how to mend her marriage. Nothing came of the latter, however, indeed nor could it after Thistlethwayte's death in August 1887. His death was the result of a self-inflicted gunshot wound, although rather than suicide this could have been the accidental consequence of his habit of summoning the couple's household staff by firing his old service revolver.

On his death his widow retired to a leafy corner of north London; when she died seven years later she left an estate worth approximately £20 million at current values. Curiously she bequeathed the total to a younger son of the 7th Duke of Newcastle in the hope that it would be used to establish a retreat for clergymen. This never happened.

48. Dame Henrietta Barnett
(1851-1936)

Hampstead Garden Suburb, NW11

There is an official Blue Plaque on her former home at Heath End House in Spaniards Road, NW3, but Dame

Henrietta's real monument is the mixed, model suburb she established with her social-reforming clergyman husband Samuel Barnett.

The idea was not her own but Ebenezer Howard's, a housing pioneer whose *Garden Cities of To-morrow* in 1898 set out the blueprint for utopian communities in which people of all classes could live in harmony with nature. His ideas were radical for the time but enormously attractive, and within five years an attempt was made at Letchworth in Hertfordshire to put some of his theories into practice.

The same year a letter to *The Times* proposed the creation of a new garden suburb immediately adjacent to Hampstead Heath and the Barnetts' own home. Dame Henrietta's interest was thus twofold. A genuine desire to provide a model community for the middle- and working-classes dovetailed neatly with a wish to halt the mindless suburbanization of London, or at least to prevent it from spreading all over the enviable, semi-rural openness of Hampstead Heath now that the railway had started running commuter services as far as Golders Green.

An early recruit to her cause was Raymond Unwin, who with Barry Parker was one of the creators of Letchworth Garden City and a friend of Canon Barnett's. As an architect and town planner he saw in her ideas the best possible opportunity to break through the multiplicity of codes and restrictions that had stifled house building in London since the Great Fire. In particular he was keen

to avoid the monotony and uniformity that characterized so many London streets, working on a large scale to
make use of the contours of the land and other natural
features, thereby creating neighbourhoods that were
human in scale and architecturally harmonious. The
farmland on which to do this, initially around 240 acres
formerly owned by Eton College, was secured through
Dame Henrietta's tireless lobbying of influential friends
and contacts.

Creating an entirely new suburb was easily her largest project, but it was far from being Henrietta Barnett's
first foray into social reform. Soon after meeting her
future husband through a mutual friend, National Trust
co-founder Octavia Hill, Henrietta found herself living
in poverty-stricken Whitechapel where Samuel Barnett
had his ministry.* Coming from a prosperous Clapham
household the squalor of the inner city appalled her
and, with no family of her own, the shock of Whitechapel
must have provided much of the impetus for what was
to be a lifetime's toil improving the lot of working-class
Londoners.

As well as establishing or promoting such organizations as Homes for Workhouse Girls, the Workers'
Educational Association, and the National Association

---

* When Sir Edwin Lutyens designed a church for her at Hampstead
Garden Suburb the dedication was to St Jude, which had been the
name of the couple's Whitechapel parish.

for the Welfare of the Feeble-Minded, Henrietta became the first woman in the country to be appointed to a government committee. From here she led a campaign in 1890 to abolish the hated Poor Law District Schools, and to improve the quality of education for London's underprivileged children.

She and Samuel were also instrumental in the creation of two invaluable London institutions that still survive today. The first of these, Toynbee Hall, was a pioneer of the Victorian settlement movement that explored practical ways for rich and poor to live more closely together. The second was the Whitechapel Gallery, one of the first publicly funded galleries intended specifically for temporary or loan exhibitions. Its milestones over the last hundred years have included the first public display in this country of Pablo Picasso's anti-war *Guernica*, and major exhibitions by artists as diverse as Mark Rothko and Nan Goldin, David Hockney and Jackson Pollock. Recently extended, the gallery continues to go from strength to strength.

With such a roster of successes Dame Henrietta could perhaps be forgiven for leaving behind each new project as she moved on to the next, but this was rarely the case. Instead she chose to remain closely involved with those whose lives she had touched, often until her dying days. A frequent visitor at the girls' school she founded, for example, the still astonishingly successful Henrietta

Barnett School, she was described as 'an amazing person, vital and alive, with a fine presence' just weeks before she died in June 1936.

49. Vincent van Gogh (1853-90)

87 Hackford Road, SW9

Good at drawing from an early age, the Dutch-born pastor's son did not become an artist until his late twenties, having failed to secure a place at university or to follow his father into the Dutch Reformed Church. Instead he entered the art world first as a salesman, a trade in which he had good family connections including three art-dealer uncles.

Aged sixteen, after a childhood that he described as 'gloomy and cold and sterile' he was apprenticed to the Hague gallery of Goupil & Cie, an important international dealership in which one of his uncles – also called Vincent – was a partner. The company was enormously successful at this time, with its headquarters in Paris and branches in London, Brussels, Berlin and Vienna as well as New York and Australia. Located to the north of Paris its workshops produced huge numbers of engraved, etched and eventually even photographic copies of paintings and replica sculptures designed to feed the growing middle-class demand for affordable art.

After three years or so, and doubtless with some intervention from 'Uncle Cent', Vincent was promoted to the London branch in 1872. This had been established at 17 Southampton Street, Covent Garden by Ernest Gambart, the promoter and publisher of many leading artists, including Edwin Landseer and Lawrence Alma-Tadema (who moved to London at his suggestion) as well as several members of the Pre-Raphaelite Brotherhood.

A PICTURE OF ILL HEALTH

Much has been made of Van Gogh's mental frailty, but he was also physically less than robust and in his short lifetime was frequently unwell. Attempts to poison himself by drinking oil paint and kerosene will have done nothing to boost the health of one described by a fellow artist as 'rather a weedy little man', and at various times he suffered heart palpitations and dizzy spells as well as more serious conditions such as syphilis and epilepsy. A sustained bout of toothache resulted in the loss of nearly a dozen teeth while affecting his right eye and his remaining (right) ear, and a habit of soaking his pillowcase in camphor failed to treat his chronic insomnia. A taste for absinthe and the cheapest wine, combined with a habit of eating very little and smoking, tended to exacerbate whatever ailed him at the time.

Van Gogh was later transferred to Paris (in 1876) but fired shortly afterwards when customers complained about his attitude. In particular he had become resentful about the treatment of art as a commodity, an admirable sentiment for the artist he would one day become but something that art dealers presumably accept and come to terms with as part of the job.

His time as a dealer thus ended badly but, according to one of his sisters-in-law, his first spell in England had been one of the few truly happy times in Vincent's life.* With lodgings in Stockwell's Hackford Road, he had found living in London expensive but he was good at his job and hoped quickly to progress. Photographs of the time show him clean-shaven with a neat white collar and tie, not at all the image we have of him today, and by the time he was twenty he was reportedly earning more than his father.

Often sporting a top hat without which, he insisted, 'you can't live in London', his letters speak well of the late-Victorian city: 'One of the nicest things I've seen here is Rotten Row in Hyde Park, which is a long, broad avenue where hundreds of ladies and gentlemen go riding. In every part of the city there are splendid parks with a wealth of flowers, such as I've seen nowhere else.' He was also

---

* After being fired from the Paris gallery he returned to England briefly to work as a language teacher in Ramsgate and then as assistant to a Methodist minister in Isleworth. The latter arose from Van Gogh's briefly held conviction that he wished to 'preach the Gospel everywhere'.

a regular visitor to Burlington House and the Dulwich Picture Gallery, and the British Museum where he signed the visitors' book in August 1874.

Writing to his younger brother Theo he even mentions Hackford Road – 'how I'd like to have you here, old chap, to see my new lodgings' – and it was while staying in this neat end-of-terrace house of the 1820s that he fell in love with his landlady's daughter, Eugénie Loyer. This passion was to affect him deeply for the rest of his life.

Drawn to the warmth and closeness that existed between the girl and her widowed mother Ursula, and contrasting this with the frigid atmosphere of his own family home, Van Gogh found Eugénie immensely attractive. It took a while but eventually Van Gogh professed his love for her, only to be rebuffed. Rejecting his advances and a proposal of marriage, Eugénie confessed that she was secretly engaged to a man called Samuel Plowman. This was another of her mother's lodgers who had earlier rented what was now Van Gogh's bedroom.[*]

The shock to Van Gogh was profound, and moving to new lodgings at 395 Kennington Road he became depressed and increasingly dispirited by his life in London. This was naturally a source of great concern to his employer and to his family, and as he spiralled downwards a transfer to Paris was arranged in the hope that he would somehow snap out of his malaise. This hope was not realized, and the offer of continued employment with Goupil & Cie was withdrawn.

Much like his career as a dealer, Van Gogh's London sojourn thus ended badly. Until his death he continued to nurse an unrequited passion for Eugénie, and while he had several significant relationships (one of them with a pregnant prostitute) he never married. But London also set him on the path to becoming an artist: early sketches taken as he crossed the river to Covent Garden, and hours spent poring over engravings of London by Doré and others in the *Illustrated London News*, contributed to the

---

[*] The two married in due course, and their descendants now live in Devon. In the early 1970s a rough, unsigned sketch in their possession was identified as being of the house in Hackford Road. After being authenticated as an original Van Gogh by a professor of art history at the University of Amsterdam it was temporarily put on display at the Barbican in London.

mix that would in time emerge as one of the great creative talents of Western art. Van Gogh famously insisted that 'one becomes a painter by painting' – but had Eugénie Loyer not rejected him, who knows whether he would even have started?

50. George Blake (1922-)

28 Highlever Road, W10

When the evening roll call at Wormwood Scrubs on 22 October 1966 revealed that the prison population was one man down, what became known as the Blake Escape made headlines around the world as news spread of the sudden disappearance of convicted British double agent George Blake.

Five years previously the Lord Chief Justice, sitting in camera at the Old Bailey, had handed down an unprecedented forty-two-year sentence when the thirty-nine-year-old was found guilty of several charges of espionage. These dated back to his time in a North Korean internment camp, a three-year spell during which Blake switched sides after reading Marx and becoming appalled by what he later described as the 'bombing of small Korean villages by enormous American Flying Fortresses'.

Released by the North Koreans in 1953 and returning home a hero, for the next nine years Blake was
employed by MI6 but stayed in regular contact with
Moscow. Typically Blake would meet his KGB handler
every three weeks, passing him useful information from
postings in Vienna, Milan and Beirut. While holding a
position in Berlin, with wonderful irony, he was specifically detailed to identify Soviet double agents.

When Blake was himself flushed out in 1961, by
Michael Goleniewski, a Polish agent who had defected
to Britain, he was immediately recalled to London. From
the start he looked certain to receive the maximum sentence for spying in peacetime, which was fourteen years.
Instead he was given three such terms to run consecu-
tively, the judge, Lord Parker of Waddington, choosing
to punish separately three different episodes in three
different countries, leaving Blake with a record sentence
for a British court and one that remained unbroken
until 1986.

Unsurprisingly there were many who were appalled at
the length of the sentence handed down to Blake, especially after the obvious but uncomfortable comparisons
were drawn between it and the much softer handling of
the more obviously middle-class and better connected
Cambridge University spies. One who found the judg-
ment completely unacceptable was Sean Bourke, who
with two anti-nuclear protesters, Michael Randle and Pat

'WORSE THAN KIM PHILBY'

The length of Blake's sentence appeared genuinely shocking at the time, but so were the impacts of his crimes – in so far as they are known. Decades later much information about the affair is still classified, and Blake himself has admitted that even he cannot recall just what he handed over 'because it was so much'.

The wrecking of Operation Gold – an audacious Anglo-American attempt to monitor communist telecoms from a secret tunnel under the Berlin Wall – was almost certainly down to him, however, while estimates of the number of friendly agents he exposed run as high as four hundred. Many of these disappeared and were almost certainly executed, leading MI6 head Dick White to hint that Blake may well have done more harm to the service and to his country than even Kim Philby.

Pottle, hatched a plan to spring Blake from prison and help him on his way to Moscow.

Their plan was carefully considered but slightly amateurish, and with no real funding it now reads more like a wacky 1960s movie caper than real life. For example, papers recently released show that MI5 considered Blake to be a model prisoner, and confirm that he was 'too closely monitored' to make a bid to escape. Yet simply by throwing a length of rope over the prison's east wall the three conspirators were able to bundle him into a waiting

Humber motor car, and spirit him away to a prearranged safe house less than half a mile away before the authorities even realized he had gone.

A suitable hideaway had been rented by Bourke, who disguised himself with plain-glass spectacles and a false beard before interviewing potential landlords. The owner of the bedsit at Highlever Road was a German, so may have been fooled by his fake English accent; but it was anyway to be only a temporary arrangement. While the three made further plans to drive Blake to East Germany in a hastily converted campervan, Blake was moved on again, this time to a former army barracks in Willow Road, NW3.

By late December it was felt safe to attempt a crossing of the English Channel, Randle and his wife planning to drive the van from Ostend to East Germany as quickly as possible. With rumours circulating that the authorities had ordered a coffin to be opened in their search for the missing spy, the two took their children along to make their adventure look more like a simple family trip. Blake was to lie concealed in a specially built compartment behind a drawer in the camper. He was also given a DIY passport that had been bodged by Randle using an old one of his own, together with a new photograph and some Plastic Padding adhesive to fake the necessary stamps.

Fortunately, as they made their way across Europe the only inspection made of the vehicle was carried out by two friendly East German border guards – but even this was fairly cursory as they said they did not wish to disturb the children. Shortly afterwards Blake was dropped at a hotel, and a few months later he was photographed enjoying a holiday with his mother in the Carpathian Mountains. Subsequently made a colonel in the KGB, as recently as 2007 President Vladimir Putin marked Blake's eighty-fifth birthday by awarding him the Order of Friendship, one of Russia's highest awards.

In 1989, in an intriguing postscript, Pottle and Randle were arrested for their part in the escape after publishing a book detailing their exploits. Bourke had died seven years previously, and deciding to defend themselves in court the pair emphatically denied condoning Blake's crimes but insisted his sentence was vicious, inhuman, unwarranted, hypocritical and unfair. The jury agreed, both were found innocent of all charges and walked free, and at the time of writing Blake is still alive and living somewhere in Russia on a full KGB pension.

INDEX

ABOUT THE AUTHOR

Writer and journalist David Long has regularly appeared in *The Times* and the *London Evening Standard*, as well as on TV and radio. He has written many popular and well-received books on London, including *Hidden City, Tunnels Towers & Temples* and the successful *A History of London in 100 Places*, which is also published by Oneworld. Find him online at www.davidlong.info.